TRUE PROSPERITY

HOW TO HAVE EVERYTHING

For further information:

The Kabbalah Centre
155 E. 48th St., New York, NY 10017
1062 S. Robertson Blvd., Los Angeles, CA 90035

1.800.Kabbalah www.kabbalah.com

First Edition
May 2005
Printed in USA
ISBN 1-57189-319-9

Design: Hyun Min Lee

TRUE PROSPERITY

HOW TO HAVE EVERYTHING

www.kabbalah.com™

BY THE AUTHOR OF 72 NAMES OF GOD

YEHUDA BERG

DEDICATION

This book is dedicated to all of you who have been so generous in your giving, especially when giving was not so easy.

The words that fill the pages of this book came easily. After all, I spent my entire life preparing to write them. When the time came, I sat at the keyboard and all I had to do was type fast enough to keep up with the powerful flow of Kabbalistic concepts that have defined my existence.

I find myself overwhelmed, unable to find the language to articulate my gratitude to the men and women who have continuously supported the mission of The Kabbalah Centre. In fact, I cannot think of a single word that coveys the deep sense of appreciation I feel for those who have directly contributed to the explosive growth of Kabbalistic wisdom in the world.

The Zohar teaches that sharing in a way that encourages others to become beings of sharing is the highest form of giving. The many men and women who direct their contributions to The Kabbalah Centre are doing just that. They are participating in something so big that it is transforming the world; and, at the same time, they are creating a place in their own lives where *true prosperity* can exist.

The manifestation of your giving has made this book possible. You are bringing Light to our world and, in turn, to your own lives.

TABLE OF CONTENTS

ACKNOWLEDGMENTS

I would like to thank the many people who have made this book possible.

First and foremost, Rav and Karen Berg, my parents and teachers. I will be forever thankful for your continual guidance, wisdom, and unconditional support. I am just one of the many whom you have touched with your love and wisdom.

Michael Berg, my brother, for your constant support and friendship, and for your vision and strength. Your presence in my life inspires me to become the best that I can be.

My wife, Michal, for your love and commitment; for your silent power; for your beauty, clarity, and uncomplicated ways. You are the strong foundation that gives me the security to soar.

David, Moshe, Channa, and Yakov, the precious gifts in my life who remind me every day how much there is to be done to ensure that tomorrow will be better than today.

Billy Phillips, one of my closest friends, for your help in making this book possible. The contribution you make to The Kabbalah Centre every day and in so many ways is appreciated far more than you could possibly know.

To Paul Wolfe for sharing your gift in the pursuit of bringing Kabbalah to the "marketplace" as *The Zohar* says, for all people to learn.

To Hyun Lee, Christian Witkin, and Esther Sibilia, whose contributions made the physical quality and integrity of everything we do live up to the spiritual heritage of this incredible wisdom that has been passed on to me by my father, Rav Berg.

I want to thank Rich Freese, Eric Kettunen, and all the team at PGW for their vision and support. Your proactive efficiency gives us the confidence to produce more and more books on Kabbalah so that the world can benefit from this amazing wisdom.

To all the Chevre at The Kabbalah Centres worldwide—the evenings we share together in study fuel my passion to bring the power of Kabbalah to the world. You are a part of me and my family no matter where you might be.

To the students who study Kabbalah all over the world —your desire to learn, to improve your lives, and to share with the world is an inspiration. The miracles I hear from you every day make everything I do worthwhile.

WHAT IS TRUE PROSPERITY?

Here's a fascinating question (or rather a few of them): Why do so many sincere people invest in books and courses on money, investing, real estate, success—and yet at the end of the day, so few people really achieve it?

Why is it that the people who make the most money out of so-called money-making courses are the people who sell the courses?

And why is it that people who actually seem to achieve success pay such a high price for it—in terms of their relationships, their families, and their health?

The answer to all these questions lies in the fact that what people truly want, deep down in the farthest reaches of their chromosomes, isn't to be successful. Instead, they want to be fulfilled. And by that I mean deeply and truly fulfilled—brimming with joy, satisfaction, prosperity, and the feeling of having earned it all.

Money by itself, even tankers full of it, is a poor substitute for that fulfillment. Sure, money is great—and don't worry, because by the time you finish this book, you'll be well on your way to having a great deal of it. But the fulfillment I'm talking about here is something I call True Prosperity.

Well, what's "untrue" prosperity?

The kind of success that usually passes for prosperity in this world is based on compromise—on having one thing but giving up another. It's success with side effects: You make a lot of money, but you give up time with your kids. Or you make even more money than that, but you're depressed because you lack serenity. Or you make oodles of money—you're practically swimming in the stuff—but you earn it by lying, cheating, stealing, and walking over a bridge built of human bodies (and you wonder why you don't sleep well at night).

None of these situations, **especially the last one**, creates true prosperity—because true prosperity is a condition in which you have **everything**. You have all the money you could ever want, **plus** the time to be a little league coach and a roving photographer at children's birthday parties. You run a business that propels itself from one success to another, but you also have joyous connections with the people in your life—your friends, your employees, your colleagues, and even your business competitors.

The secret is that true prosperity is really what each of us was put on earth to achieve. And that's the key word here: **achieve**. You achieve prosperity not because you're smart or lucky, or because you so ruthlessly pillaged your competition, but because you followed the rules of the universe.

THE RULES OF THE UNIVERSE FOR HARD-HEADED BUSINESS TYPES

If you look at life as a business, the original business plan can be said to have been written 4000 years ago by a group of ancient business consultants known as kabbalists. And their plan, which is now contained in the world's oldest wisdom—Kabbalah—unraveled the mysteries of life and of the universe. It explained in detail the spiritual and physical laws that govern the human soul. That's quite a business plan! And if "mysteries of life" and discussions of the soul sound like religion to you, bear in mind that numerous scientific giants throughout history would beg to differ.

Pythagoras studied Kabbalah. Sir Isaac Newton's Zohar—the principal text of Kabbalah—now sits under glass at Oxford University. Gottfried Leibniz, who introduced calculus to the world, considered Kabbalah the blueprint to reality. Philosophers of the Age of Enlightenment in Europe found within the teachings of Kabbalah a pure fountain of long-lost ancient wisdom.

So what makes this book different is that it's not just another book about making money that offers some insights and then sends you on your way.

To the contrary, this book is a gift!

It is a personal gift to all of us from those ancient business consultants, the kabbalists, who want your business to soar and your life to soar along with it. They would like to present you with an array of kabbalistic technologies—tools that you can apply now and every second of your life, not only in your financial life but in your personal life as well (both of which are closely intertwined). So what is Kabbalah?

Kabbalah, which literally means *RECEIVE*, is about having it all!

So let's put Pythagoras, Newton, Leibniz, and scientific explorations aside. Our aim here is not to create a new theory of the cosmos; it's to change your life with a new dimension of prosperity. It's to help you escape from "business as usual"—a realm in which 90% of startup businesses fail; in which people keep leaving their jobs or are asked to do so; and in which those who actually stay employed view their jobs as some unique form of punishment that has been devised expressly for them.

There is a better way of doing business—and of doing life. And though the wisdom of Kabbalah dates back to Abraham as well as to a highly esoteric work called the *Book of Formation*, that wisdom can reach right into your business today, at the desk where you are sitting, striving to earn a living, to better yourself, and to make a better life for your family. The kabbalistic tools that we will explore will teach you how to win the game of business and finance and, in the process, win the game of life.

So what is the game about?

THE ULTIMATE BUSINESS PLAN: BOSS, NOT FLUNKY

Kabbalah tells us that there is a plan that has been ingeniously devised for each person on earth, and it's not simply about being wealthy or powerful or a famous rock star. It's far more profound than that.

The purpose of this game is for each person to be the creator in his or her own universe—to become the *cause* in one's life and not the *effect* of it. It means being the proactive creator of your destiny rather than remaining condemned to react passively to each new episode of chaos that comes along.

It means that if life is a business, you're the boss, not the flunky.

Kabbalists also suggest that you are here because you asked to be—**which means that you devised the original business plan yourself!**

You asked to be here, in this world of pain and suffering and chaos, and then you forgot. You lived in perfection, in a paradise of endless light, and you chose to come here—and then you forget that you ever made that decision in the first place!

Stay with me here.

Because even if you claim that you can't remember having made any such decision, bear this in mind: If you can't remember what you had for lunch a year and a half ago, let alone the blissful nine-month vacation you once spent in your mother's womb, it stands to reason that you don't remember the cosmic womb you inhabited before you descended into earthly existence.

The question is, why did you decide to come here in the first place?

EVERY SINGLE SHARE OF MICROSOFT STOCK—YOURS FREE

You had the joy and bliss of what kabbalists call the Endless World handed to you with no effort. In business terms, it was like having every share of Microsoft Corporation awarded to you on a heavenly platter.

But you turned down the offer!

Instead, you decided to relocate your business to a harsh, dark world beset with pain and problems - to a life that Shakespeare once described as "a tale told by an idiot, full of sound and fury, signifying nothing."

But why?

We'll begin our explanation with a little story.

Dad is a successful entrepreneur, and over the course of a stellar career he's built a highly profitable business. Having come of age, his son decides to enter the family business, where he works hard and climbs the corporate ladder—going from mailroom assistant to division head and finally to second in command. But at a party that is held to celebrate his promotion, a harsh truth is revealed to the young man: All along, his father had paid the firm's employees to make his son look good. They were all part of a scheme that had been devised to make it look as though the son was doing a great job, when in fact he had never really accomplished anything at all. It was a foregone conclusion that one day the son would be named second in command, so his life at the company had been nothing more than a charade.

How does the son feel upon hearing this news?

Well, how would *you* feel?

That's right: stunned and disappointed.

So it isn't really the position or the power itself that brings fulfillment, is it? Something deep within us is programmed by divine nature to need to *earn* what we get before we can truly enjoy it. We need to be the cause in our life, not the effect.

The Creator invented this game to give each of us a chance to be the cause and creator of our own universe, and true prosperity lies in accomplishing just that. It's about meeting challenges head on and coming out on top. It's about putting the pieces of the puzzle together ourselves rather than being handed the final product.

Kabbalists explain that you came here in order to experience what it means to be the Creator. You chose to become a proactive participant in the construction of your own paradise. You didn't want the family business handed over to you by Dad; you wanted to earn it yourself, because you knew that only in the earning would you find true fulfillment.

And there's that word again—*fulfillment.* The fulfillment of true prosperity.

So that's the purpose of the game. But before we begin, let's take a look at how the game was constructed.

ENTER YOUR ULTIMATE COMPETITOR

Picture this, if you will: Michael Jordan never sees the inside of a basketball court. Instead, he whiles away his time in his own backyard all by himself, dribbling his basketball and idly scoring one basket after another.

Picture this: An angel descends and hands you a magical golf club. With this club, your ball soars into the hole every time you tee off, no matter what the course conditions might be. You score a hole in one on every shot, time after time after time.

Picture this: Timmy closes his eyes excitedly while playing a game of hide-and-seek. He can't wait to open them so that he can run around the yard and find where his friends are hidden. But when he finally does open his eyes, lo and behold, there are no hiding places to be found. His friends are all just standing there, staring at him.

In this alternate reality, would Michael Jordan ever have become the greatest basketball player of all time? Would you ever have roused yourself from a delicious slumber at 6 A.M. to play a nice round of golf? Would Timmy have had the time of his life playing hide-and-seek?

Clearly not, because in each of these scenarios there is something missing.

There is no Opponent!

THE ULTIMATE COMPETITOR

When there is no Opponent, there is no game. Think about it: Without an Opponent, you have no opportunity to challenge yourself and to become great—greater than you ever dreamed you could be, and certainly greater than you could possibly become just by hanging out by yourself.

Without an Opponent, Michael Jordan would just be a guy throwing balls at a hoop. Without an Opponent (in this case, space and gravity and the resistance of your own body), golf would just be a walk in a meadow with a stick in your hand. Without an Opponent, Timmy would just be a kid standing around looking at his friends.

Without an Opponent, there is no challenge, no purpose, no fun.

And there is no opportunity to **earn fulfillment**.

In order to have a game, there has to be an Opponent— and in the game of life, we have a magnificent one indeed. Our insidiously powerful Opponent has been provided to us free of charge by the Commander of the Universe, better known as the Creator, or God. And the Opponent has been provided to us for one purpose only: to allow us to overcome him, thereby becoming the cause and not the effect in our lives.

But this isn't some namby-pamby Opponent we're facing here. Oh no, the Creator knows exactly what He is doing. To help us become the boss and not the flunky in the business of life, the Creator has provided an around-the-clock, never-resting, cutthroat competitor who is hell-bent on seeing us fail.

Let's call him the *Ultimate Competitor*.

Kabbalists have a term for the Ultimate Competitor. They call him Satan, pronounced suh-*tan*. But the word has woven itself into our cultural imagination to such an extent that when we think of Satan, we conjure up a guy in a bright red suit, complete with pitchfork and horns. But the Competitor is not like that at all. Indeed, there's no guy, no pitchfork, no horns, and no purgatory await-ing us if we're bad. In fact, in its original kabbalistic translation, the word *Satan* actually means *adversary*.

The Competitor is a negative force in the universe that pushes us unceasingly toward chaos.

The Competitor is scheming 24/7 to devise ways to ruin you and to run you out of business. But the truly fright-ening part of it is that he's not working across town or even down the street from you. Instead, he operates inside your skull. **The Competitor lives inside of you!**

Kabbalists long ago observed that our true enemy—our Opponent—cannot be found among the people we meet in business or run across in the course of our everyday lives. To the contrary, our true Competitor dwells within us—and from this perch, he thinks our thoughts and speaks in our voice. He distracts us and forces us to lose focus. He makes sure we operate like puppets, reacting in a robotic fashion to all the events in our lives—because when you react rather than act, you are merely a puppet, an effect. And when you're an effect rather than a cause in your life, fulfillment can never be yours. Instead, you will labor for success but will sacrifice human assets for financial ones. Hey, if you make the money, you can't make the birthday parties, right?

That's the Competitor speaking.

If we make successful mergers at the office, we divorce at home. Money or love—they're mutually exclusive, right?

That's him speaking again.

And it gets worse.

YOU CHASE YOUR TAIL, AND THEN YOU DIE

Instead of true prosperity, the Competitor works to ensure our downfall. Look at it this way: Suppose we come into the world programmed with a preset desire. Let's say that our desire is to earn $1000. So we harness our energies, do the work, and *voilà*: $1000. But then what does the Competitor do? He goads us into playing double or nothing. And now we feel that we must earn another $2000; we can't rest, because we feel we'll be total failures unless we earn it. So we focus on that $2000 to the exclusion of all else. "Sorry, honey, I can't make the party at the Millers'," we say. Or "Not now, Jason, I'm on the phone." Or "Alex, can you take Emmy to school? I have paperwork to finish." Of course, when we finally obtain the $2000, we know what the Competitor will do: He will play double or nothing once again.

So we spend our lives chasing something we never attain, at the expense of everything else!

Kids, friends, peace of mind—all are sacrificed to this meaningless, robotic, continual game of double or nothing. This is the job of our Opponent, our Ultimate Competitor. And if we follow this path, we will ultimately leave the world unfulfilled, empty, and sad—because no matter what we have accomplished, **we will have fulfilled only half of our desires!**

IN A ZERO-SUM GAME, YOU END UP
WITH ZERO

This, then, is the world according to the Competitor: Business life and family life are separate, and never the twain shall meet. You can be nice and loving at home; you can work hard to be a devoted husband and a fun and energetic dad; and you can try not to be selfish or angry. But set one foot inside the office, and all bets are off. There you can explode with anger, treat people like dirt, ruthlessly pursue success, step on people, and kill before you yourself are killed. Hey, that's business, you say! It's you against them.

The business model of the Competitor is a zero-sum game. His universe is one of scarcity and lack, not abundance. If one person gains, another must lose. If John gets the promotion, you won't. If Acme International gets the account, then your pitch will be turned down.

In the world of the Competitor, money is not the great equalizer; it's the great separator. It separates people from people, colleagues from colleagues, employers from employees. And within each person's heart, it separates one's financial life from one's personal life. In it there are limits—limits to goodness, to wealth, to opportunity. We're not in this together; we're in this separately.

But Kabbalah has a word for this insidious scenario: **bogus!**

It is a recipe for ruin, and one that has been devised by a business consultant who, rather than leading you to true fulfillment and true prosperity, is leading you to chaos—better known as the Suddenly Syndrome.

SUDDENLY, SUDDENLY, SUDDENLY . . .

In business as usual, things happen *suddenly*.

Does that ring true in your life?

Suddenly, an investment goes south. Suddenly, the market turns down. Suddenly, your favorite employee quits—or is indicted. Suddenly you have health problems or cash-flow problems. Suddenly you're in the wrong place at the wrong time with the wrong product.

Kabbalah exposes this Suddenly Syndrome as an illusion—for in fact, nothing ever happens suddenly. We inhabit a cause-and-effect universe, not a *suddenly* universe. Everything in the world is an effect of some cause; although it may take ten minutes or ten days or ten lifetimes to manifest, every action will eventually have an effect. If you think someone "suddenly" got cancer, ask a doctor, and he will tell you that the malignancy began developing in the body many years before it was finally diagnosed.

The tools of kabbalistic technology can free you from business as usual, from the Competitor as usual, from chaos as usual. In like manner, these tools can free you from all the inexplicable reasons your business might have failed—why you just happened not to get the information you needed about the market. It can free you from the illusion of *suddenly*. And even better, seeing through the eyes of kabbalistic wisdom can turn your greatest enemy into your greatest friend, putting the negative power of the Competitor to a positive purpose.

THE POWER OF "X"

Once, a young man washed up on the shores of America, one of thousands of Eastern European immigrants searching for a better life. Soon he landed a job in a clothing store as an assistant to an assistant to an assistant. The young man's entire job consisted of taking sales receipts, signing them, and then handing them to his boss. But the man couldn't speak English, so instead of signing his name on these receipts, he marked each of them with an "X."

When the young man's boss saw the X's, he looked quizzically at the employee, realized he couldn't speak a word of English, and fired him on the spot.

Now we flash forward to 30 years later. The scene is a sleek boardroom on the 50th floor of a gleaming new office building. A deal worth hundreds of millions of dollars is being transacted, and one of the businessmen is signing the contract. His colleagues notice that he has signed with an "X" rather than with his name, and they ask him why.

"I have signed every contract in my career with an 'X,' " the man replies. "It always reminds me that if I hadn't signed some papers with an 'X' many years ago, I would still be the assistant to an assistant to an assistant in a clothing store."

Like the kabbalist, this business tycoon sees beyond the Opponent's goals to the purpose the Opponent serves for us. It is the same purpose that was served by the boss who fired that young immigrant who couldn't speak English—the same purpose served by the NBA stars who challenged Michael Jordan on his every ascent to the basket. And it is the same purpose served by the golf course in which there is so much grass and so little hole.

The Creator created the Opponent—the Competitor— for the sole purpose of allowing us to overcome him and, in the process, experience the joy of triumph. In this way we can be the cause, not just the effect. And in this way you can be the boss in the business of your life, not just the flunky.

Now, just a word of caution . . .

A word of caution must be added about being the boss.

When we call someone *boss*, it sounds as though they're pretty special—they are the king or the queen, and everyone is waiting on them hand and foot. They are in charge; people kowtow to them, and all the profit that is made is theirs to keep. But this is the Competitor speaking, and there is a major piece of trickery taking place.

The Competitor is hiding himself in something we all have, and something that derails us from ever having true fulfillment. And that disguise is . . .

Ego

A code word for the Competitor is ego. The road that leads businesses and lives to go belly-up has a neon sign flashing with three letters: E-G-O.

Hidden in the word *ego* is this phrase: **E**veryone's **G**ot **O**ne.

Ego is an amazingly overused word, but kabbalistically it stands for something very clear: It stands for an illusion, a fake self. It stands for a false notion of who we are and what we are entitled to. And as long as we go to work, run our business, and interact with family and friends in the throes of this illusion, chaos and frustration are bound to greet us at every turn.

Ego is at work when you have an inflated view of yourself, but it's also at work when you have a deflated view of yourself. Ego is a condition not unlike depression, and when we are in it, we are cut off from everyone and everything around us.

Ego is wrong not because it's evil or because it isn't nice, but because it's a lie. Like a steel curtain, it cuts us off from the truth that is the source of all wealth, health, prosperity, and fulfillment.

But if ego is a curtain, what it's blocking is the fundamental reality of the universe—something Kabbalah calls . . .

The Light.

AND NOW FOR THE TRUTH

We call this place in which we live *the world*. Look around and there it is. We don't question it very much; our eyes see it, our noses smells it, our ears hear it, and our fingers touch it. This book you're reading is part of the world, as is the chair you're sitting on, the itch on your back, and Tom Cruise's private jet. They're all part of a vast fabric called material reality—or, as some would call it, "the real world."

But kabbalists have some news about all this—if insights dating back thousands of years can be said to be news.

What kabbalists saw 4000 years ago . . .

and quantum physicists saw in the 1900s . . .

and Superstring Theory now confirms is that . . .

Reality isn't what it's cracked up to be.

In fact, reality isn't even real, despite the evidence of our senses. It is a world that appears real purely *because of* the limitations of our perceptions.

Okay, so you wanted to find out how to get wealthy, and now I'm telling you that reality isn't even real. How is that going to lead you to prosperity? Don't worry, there is a connection—and when you make that connection, you will find out where true abundance and wealth lie.

So stick around!

As I was saying when I interrupted myself, all that you see, hear, smell, taste, and touch makes up only 1% of the universe. "Mother Nature is having a double laugh," space scientist Bruce Margon once commented. "She's hidden most of the matter in the universe, and hidden it in a form that can't be seen."

In fact, 99% of the universe is unseen, unheard, and unperceived. So let's call our everyday, physical world the 1% reality. And let's call the spiritual world—the world of thoughts and consciousness and Light—the 99% world.

The 99% realm happens to be the source of all energy, consciousness, and creativity. In fact, the 1% world is really an illusion; it is a shadow of the 99% world. Nothing exists in the 1% world that doesn't have the 99% realm as its source.

THE INFINITE DATABASE OF WHAT ISN'T

Mozart sits down, and when he gets up, he dashes off the entire score of the opera *Don Giovanni* in one sitting.

A business student comes up with an idea for an overnight package-delivery business. It earns him only a C in his class, but when he graduates, he starts the business. He calls it "Federal Express."

A successful filmmaker decides to turn his films into reality by creating a cross between a carnival, a world's fair, and the cartoon world of his movies. Not a single investor wants to invest a dime in this vision, but Walt Disney pursues his idea anyway. He calls it "Disneyland."

Each of these ideas came from the 99% realm. Every act of creation, from the humblest notion to the ideas that have changed the world (or that jump-start your business), has arisen because somehow, someone plugged into the 99% world. Someone emerged from the realm of the five senses—the realm of what already is—and accessed the infinite database of what isn't.

1% PROSPERITY VS. 99% PROSPERITY

So let's summarize these laws of the universe.

In the physical realm, you have chaos, struggle, and conflict. In place of creative breakthroughs, you have repetition of what's already been done. You have a life that is lived reactively, as an effect of the outside world—as flunky rather than boss.

In the 99% realm, on the other hand, you have fulfillment, joy, true creativity, and peace that endures. You are connected to what kabbalists call the Light of the Creator. It is this realm that is hidden from us both by the Competitor and by our ego nature. Yet it is the only place that truly empowers us to be the boss of our own lives.

Just as there are two realms to which you can connect, so too are there two kinds of prosperity. First there's the 1% kind of prosperity, where you get money but not love. It is here that businesses rise fast and fall even faster, and you have no idea why. And it is here that emergencies happen . . . *suddenly.*

Then there's the 99% kind of prosperity, in which you have not only money but a life that actually lets you enjoy it. Your life is blessed with love, health, happiness, and true satisfaction.

At every moment of your life, you choose which realm you connect to. Connect to the 1% realm and you're the flunky, chasing false prosperity with limited thinking. Connect to the 99% realm and you become the boss, opening the door to true prosperity.

And this brings us to money. You've heard of money, right? But what *is* money, really?

MONEY IS LIGHT!

That's the kabbalistic secret of money. Money isn't a thing; money is energy. Money is Light.

This certainly shatters conventional notions of money. Have you noticed how money sometimes seems a bit suspect, more than a little unsavory? Often we feel as if it comes with a tinge of guilt around the edges. Spirituality and money can't legally cohabit, can they? "I have to earn money," you might say, "but it isn't spiritual; it's kind of a necessary evil. To be truly spiritual, well, you have to hop on a plane for Tibet and meditate on a mountaintop, don't you?"

Kabbalah teaches that this paradigm of money is simply **wrong!**

And it is wrong for totally scientific reasons.

Money is energy, so how can energy be bad? Is electricity bad? Well, use it to light your bungalow, and it's good. But stick your finger in a wall socket, and it's definitely bad. In both cases, it's the same electricity. It's simply how you have harnessed it that's different.

Money is energy, and like all energy, more is better. But energy, like the sun, comes with a warning label. Walk hand in hand with your children in the glow of a Tahitian sunrise and it's wonderful. But gaze at the morning sun after dwelling in a cave for 12 years and you'll likely go blind. It's the not the sun that has changed in each case; it's your relationship to it.

The Government Agrees! Money is Not Physical

Money is energy, and if that ever becomes unclear to you, the U.S. Government will gladly remind you of it. In the 1960s, the government liberated the dollar from that inconvenient thing known as the gold standard. You remember the gold standard, right? You used to be able to take a dollar bill and buy a dollar's worth of gold with it. But this is no longer the case. Today, a dollar is solely a representation of the health of the American economy. It is something spiritual, a symbol of confidence. Money is energy.

YOU WON THE LOTTERY! SORRY

This, then, is the astounding truth: **There is nothing physical about money anymore.** Money is 99%, not 1%. Money is consciousness.

A stock trader on Wall Street worth $50 million loses half his fortune in one day, when the market crashes and causes his net worth to fall to $25 million. Meanwhile, on that same day, a mailman in Wichita sells a stock short and doubles his $10,000 savings to $20,000.

Who goes to bed that night with peace of mind and a deeper sense of security and fulfillment—the stock trader, with his $25 million, or the mailman, with his $20,000?

Money is not physical.

When you use money to share—to make things grow, to bring great projects into the world, to provide for your family—it will be a force for good. But if it falls into your life unearned and undeserved, and if you keep it to satisfy your egotistic desires, it can destroy you.

And if you think money is something to be avoided, money will, at the end of the day, avoid you.

The universe as a whole functions like an electrical circuit: As long as the current flows, electricity is good. But if you overload your circuit, you can easily burn it out.

Money obeys the same law: When your attitude toward money is healthy, it will flow and bring you prosperity— and if you move on to help others gain that same prosperity, more will follow. But stop the flow at any time, and the overload can be disastrous.

You may be holding a winning lottery ticket in your pocket right now, but that may not be a good thing. Studies of lottery winners have repeatedly shown that a sudden avalanche of unearned cash can lead to disaster— not to the idyllic, fairy-tale life depicted in the commercials.

In fact, if you want to read true tales of tragedy, forget the unemployed, the sick, and the abandoned. Instead, just read about the folks who have won megamillions at games of chance. Take, for example, the true story of Jack (not his real name), who won $16.2 million in the Pennsylvania state lottery.

A former girlfriend successfully sued Jack for a share of his winnings.

Jack's brother was arrested for hiring a hit man to kill him, hoping to inherit a share of Jack's winnings.

Jack's siblings hounded him until he agreed to invest in a car business and a restaurant in Sarasota, Florida, both of which never earned a dime and severely strained his relationship with his family.

Jack himself spent time in jail for firing a gun over the head of a bill collector.

Within one year, he was $1 million in debt.

"I wish it had never happened," Jack said. "It was totally a nightmare."

He now lives on Social Security.

When vast amounts of unearned dollars fall into the hands of someone who is just scraping by—someone with no consciousness of money as energy, as abundance, as circuitry—it harks back to our long-time cave dweller, who suddenly walked out of his cave and stared directly into the blinding sun.

If you are the effect of money rather than its cause—if you have money but did not earn it—you simply cannot enjoy it. This is a kabbalistic rule of the universe, and it has a special name . . .

BREAD OF SHAME

The kabbalistic term *Bread of Shame* comes down to us from ancient times. There once was a rich man and a poor man, and the rich man kept giving money to the poor man—giving, giving, and giving. Meanwhile, the poor man kept taking from the rich man—taking, taking, and taking. Finally, rather than feeling gratitude, the poor man began to resent the rich man. Eventually, he hated him.

Remember, our world was created so that we could be the cause and not the effect. The purpose of its existence is to provide a laboratory in which we can earn our joy and fulfillment. So while you may well be daydreaming about lottery tickets hitting and rich uncles departing, be forewarned that receiving money without having earned it simply doesn't work. That which you don't earn won't satisfy you and will eventually become contaminated. Money has energy, and through Bread of Shame, that energy can become corrupted.

The DNA of Money

DNA is the instruction manual for our cells. Our cells begin in an undifferentiated state, and it is our DNA that decides which becomes a liver cell, which a brain cell, and which a skin cell. But as we live, our DNA gets corrupted. According to Kabbalah, we could continue to enjoy flawless health and could even be immortal, but our ego-driven, reactive behavior corrupts our DNA, and its instructions then get twisted. Rather than telling the cells to hum along in health, it tells them to die—and so we age, and we ourselves die.

The same principle applies to money. Remember, money is energy. So when there is Light in your money, your money will grow. And when you recognize that it is the Light that helped you earn that money—that it's not your business to hoard it but rather to keep it circulating by building others' prosperity as well as your own—then the DNA of that money will remain healthy.

When we operate with 1% consciousness—with ego consciousness—the DNA will be corrupted. And it is then that even a billion dollars can disappear overnight. In point of fact, history has recorded numerous family fortunes that have done just that—for in the end, **money without Light disappears.** The Opponent doesn't care if you have stashed it in a numbered account in Switzerland and have hidden the keys at the bottom of Lake Geneva. He has access to every penny you earn, and he can make money disappear as quickly as it appeared.

Conversely, when you plug into the 99% realm—or *Light consciousness*—your business can only go from good to better. You won't settle for 15 minutes of fame, and you won't be a one-hit wonder—because with Light consciousness, the limits are gone. Opportunities will come out of hiding and will emerge from the woodwork. A perfect stranger sitting next to you on a train will turn out to have the answer to all your problems. Life will be exciting; every moment will be precious; and every dollar you earn will be hard won.

With 1% consciousness, you become complacent. You start taking people for granted, and you take money for granted as well. And money that goes unappreciated, like a friend neglected, soon leaves.

But the perfect antidote to complacency is . . .

SURVIVOR CONSCIOUSNESS

One of the most powerful tools for achieving true prosperity is survivor consciousness. This is the state of mind that makes it possible for people to overcome even the most unspeakable of horrors; it's that hunger for life that you find in survivors of the Holocaust death camps, or the killing fields of Cambodia or Rwanda. You see it in refugees who trudge through miles of snow-covered mountain passes to cross the border to freedom before it closes, and in soldiers who have survived the terrors of wartime and come home with an indomitable desire to make something of their lives.

People who possess survivor consciousness are literally unstoppable. As a child, Roger Bannister survived a terrible fire, but his legs were so badly burned that doctors told him he'd never walk again. Not only did he prove his doctors wrong, but he became the first human being to run a four-minute mile. How many times has Donald Trump gone bankrupt and emerged more successful than before? Steve Jobs may have been pushed out of Apple, but he used his exodus to found Pixar, and he then came back to Apple to lead the company to new heights of prosperity and creativity.

But survivor consciousness isn't limited only to those who have succeeded in a trial by fire. Howard Hughes was born to great wealth, but his desire to create something new would not be denied. Survivor consciousness is a state of mind in which you feel as if your life were hanging in the balance, and spiritually speaking it is—for if you stop growing spiritually, you die.

You may be lucky enough to have been born with survivor consciousness, but if you aren't, you need to develop it. Sure, you can wait until a disaster forces you to become a survivor or, once again, you can be the cause; you can *develop* the sense that everything hangs in the balance. To do this, you need only realize that everything —not just spirituality—really does hang in the balance. What you do today will determine your tomorrow. Taking responsibility for your tomorrow keeps you hungry to make the very best choice, now, and in every moment of your life. It's that simple. Yet this simple knowledge is tremendously powerful. Keep yourself in this state, and you will be unstoppable.

You're The Boss. You're Responsible

When you're busy with the 1% world and something goes wrong, you don't say, "It's my responsibility; I am the reason for this." Instead, your response is, "Why me?"

We know that human beings in their present state are slightly imperfect—so when a negative situation arises, it would hardly be difficult for us to find, say, 30 different reasons we ourselves might have played a role in creating our problem. But this is not our usual response. Instead, the overwhelming response to the problems we face is to leap into victim consciousness by proclaiming, **It's not my fault.** The outside world is doing it to me, you say. It's the economy; it's my partners. It's the bad job market; it's the weather. What, then, is the mantra of victim consciousness? It is *Why me?* And what is the philosophy of victim consciousness? Denial. "This can't happen to me," you say. "What could I have done?"

In Light consciousness, by contrast, you respond to a negative event by saying, "I'm the boss in the business of my life, so I am responsible for everything, period. No matter what happens, if something goes wrong, it means that somewhere there was a cause, and this is the effect. Maybe I can't see how, but somewhere I must have caused it, so I can change it."

The mantra of Light consciousness? *I am responsible.* The philosophy? Embrace it and don't run from it; see what can be learned. This is happening for a reason, and it's up to me to discover that reason. I understand it and accept it, so I must move on and keep improving myself.

Let's say your agency loses a $100 million account. Do you have the strength to say, "Great—this opens the door to a $400 million account, because now we'll work 2000% instead of just 100%"?

This, then, is the kabbalistic business plan for all bosses: Take responsibility for everything that happens to you. It's as simple as that—take responsibility even for things you're not responsible for. Whether you own a company or run a department or answer the switchboard—wherever you may be in the hierarchy of your business—understand that anything that happens at one point in the structure will affect the structure as a whole. It's like those human pyramids that you see in the circus, with ten strong men forming a human triangle of support. Every person must take responsibility for the whole pyramid, because each of the ten is as important as the other: without any one of them at a given moment, there is no pyramid.

Taking responsibility helps break two of the strongest chains the Competitor uses to wrap you in: the chain of routine thinking and the chain of guilt.

EXIT NOW FROM THE ROUTINE

God may be in the details, as they say, but the Competitor is in the routine. He loves keeping you imprisoned there, doing the same things day after day— living in the same house, toiling at the same job, taking the same 5:35 train home every day. He loves seeing you revolving on the hamster wheel inside your cage. And while that cage may well have 5000 square feet, a huge swimming pool, and two perfectly manicured acres of land, it is a cage nonetheless.

The cage of which I am speaking is routine thinking, and it is what is keeping you from being like the Light, the Creator, and the cause of your own destiny. But the moment you question whether you're really happy, you start to rattle that cage. The moment you start to plug into the Light, the Competitor starts shaking. And the moment you become aware that you have a choice, you become the cause, and you can choose to be run by your routine or not.

Light consciousness is liberation from the straitjacket of the ordinary, the expected, and the logical.

And with it, everything changes.

In Light consciousness, you'll have no idea how it happens, but you'll somehow find yourself at the right place at the right time. You know those days when everything just seems to work out? Days when you tell your partner you need a software designer who runs QXV459X (whatever that is), and then some guy who made the wrong turn wanders into your office looking for the men's-room key, sees your company name, and announces that he's the inventor of QXV459X and is looking for a job? Well, in Light consciousness, you get a lot more of those days.

And you know those times when the fax machine breaks and the client calls that very second and says that they want to give you a new assignment, but first you'll have to read the pages they just faxed to you? And then your son calls to tell you that he's stranded at school because his ride didn't show up, and at that very moment your best salesperson walks up to you and says, "Just wanted to let you know, Chet, I'm leaving the company." Well, in Light consciousness, you get a lot fewer of those days.

In Light consciousness, lightbulbs begin going off, and great ideas are "suddenly" born. The jeans you just happen to be selling are the ones every kid wants to buy. You live as though the next big idea is just around the corner, because it is—and you know that the idea will show up in the place you least expect it to, falling from the lips of the last person you'd expect to hear it from. All this is Light consciousness.

In the normal course of business, companies pay millions of dollars to create those logo-and-identity programs you never notice. Nike once had a logo designed for them in the shape of a little swoosh. It cost them all of $75. I don't know for certain if Nike was plugged into Light consciousness at the time, but Kabbalah tells us that this is precisely what happens in Light consciousness. No business school can teach it to you, and there are no master's degree programs in it, at least not in universities. But it doesn't take years of study.

When you are the cause in your life and not the effect, you escape the trap of routine thinking. You realize that everything and everyone counts. You recognize that there are no accidents or coincidences; everything has a reason, because everything is connected. It all comes down to this: The Light wants you to grow, to take back your life, and to become the cause in your universe.

Quantum physics proved many years ago that our everyday perception of the world as discontinuous is an illusion. There is a quantum connection between everything, and it is in that quantum connection that true prosperity can be found.

NOT GUILTY

Guilt is the weapon of the Competitor—the weapon that makes you feel unworthy of wealth and abundance. Who are *you*, after all? You come from a small town in Idaho, and everyone you grew up with works in a rubber gasket factory. So what right do you have to enjoy a huge income, not to mention the rest of your life? There are millions of people in the world who face starvation, and people die in squalor every day. So what makes you entitled to fulfillment?

This is 1% consciousness at work. This is Competitor-grade low self-esteem. But rather than fall prey to it, you must embrace the positive as firmly as you embrace the negative. If you are wealthy, you were chosen. This is a cause-and-effect universe, so anything you have, you have earned. Somewhere and at some time, you connected to the Light—to the source—by being the source and cause in your own life. You went with Light consciousness, and abundance has come your way.

Do you deserve it? You are meant to have so much more! You deserve fulfillment beyond anything you might conceive. Each of us does.

So it's time to claim that abundance. We know that the meaning of life is to become the boss, to be the cause and not the effect. The job is to plug into Light consciousness rather than into the 1%.

Okay, so how do we do it?

Your ancient business consultants, the kabbalists, have crafted a wide variety of tools that can help you transform your nature, rise above ego consciousness, and gain true prosperity—more money than you'll know what to do with, and more joy and happiness as well.

These tools are spiritual strategies.

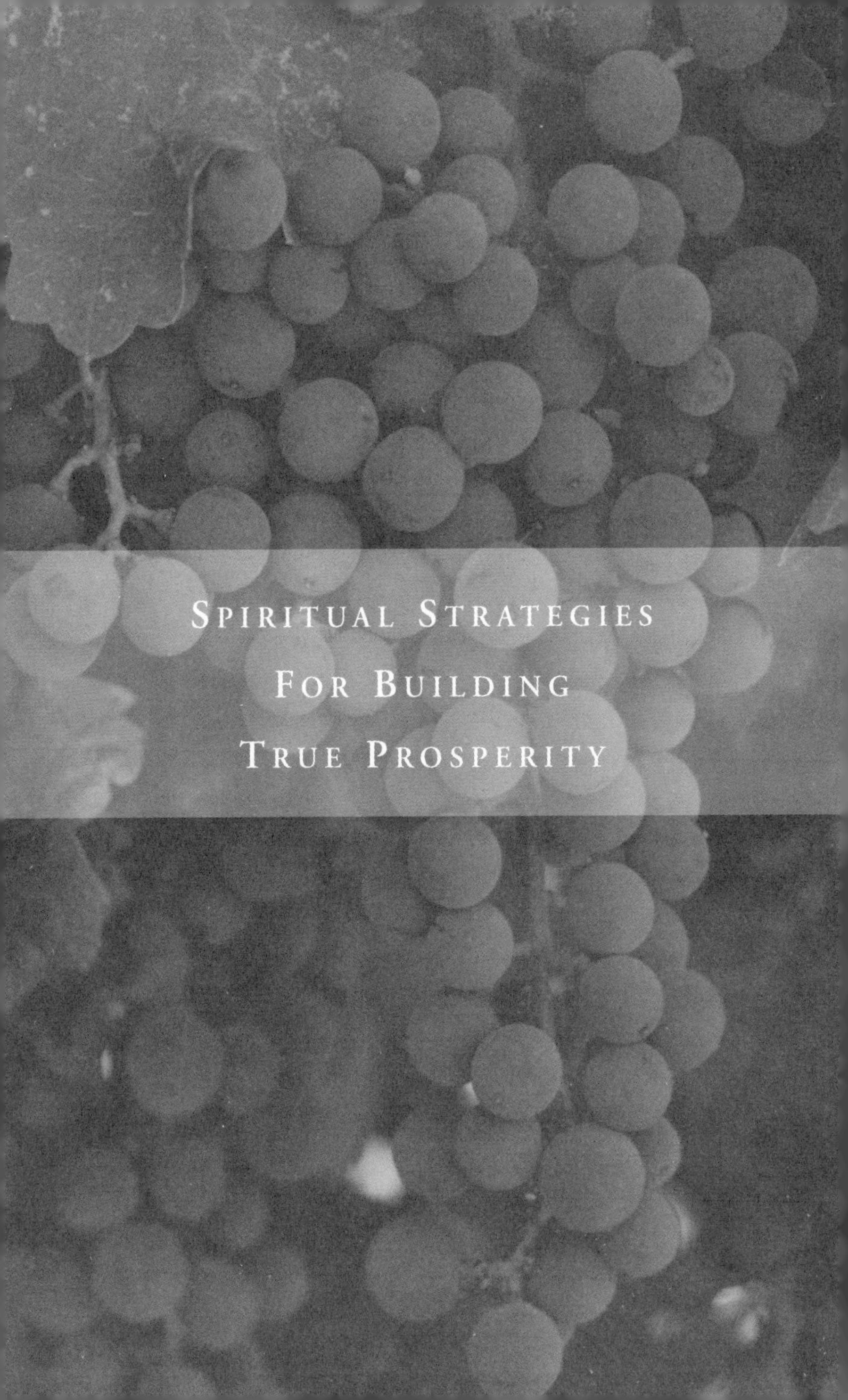

Spiritual Strategies For Building True Prosperity

HAVE GOALS, BUT REMEMBER:
THE GOALS ARE NOT THE GOALS

It has been said that a goal is a dream with a deadline. I love that description. A goal is like a promise you make to the higher part of you; it is a demarcation in space to which you commit your energy. In business, goals are the driving force on the road to prosperity—but in Kabbalah, goals are looked upon a bit differently.

One percent consciousness is your everyday, conventional way of thinking. In it, there is no cause and effect, and you operate solely from ego. In 1% consciousness, you become obsessed with your goal to the point at which the goal becomes everything. "I'll sacrifice anything to get there," you might say. "Relationships, my kids, my health

—I'm oblivious to all of them. All that exists is my goal."
Needless to say, the result of your activity will be success
with side effects. How many very wealthy people do you
know who have deep, satisfying relationships with their
partners, kids, and parents?

In Kabbalah you set goals, but the goals are not about the
goals. The goals are more like the net in a tennis match:
They force you to make a great shot, but the game isn't
about the net. It's about the tennis itself.

As you build prosperity, your goals are tools that can be
used to motivate, inspire, and move you along—to help
define the structure of the game. "I want to make
$100,000 over the next year, or $100 million," you
might say. Or "I want to have my own business, and I
want to see it flourish within three years." Or "I want to
quit my job at the accounting firm and write romance
novels." Set long- and short-term goals, but don't get lost
in them. Be ready to change them, because when you are
the boss in your life, you put your trust in the Light—
and though you may not know exactly where the Light
wants to take you, you don't worry about it. Invariably,
you know that it will be the right place.

Now it's time to discuss ego again. Ego is definitely bad,
right?

Well, yes . . . and no.

Ego. Use The Power For Good

Ego serves as the handcuffs—and *mind cuffs*—of the Competitor.

You might recall that ego is a curtain that blocks us from the Light. And what an ingenious curtain it is! Not only does it block the Light, but it is invisible—so it's not just the Light we can't see; we can't even see the curtain that blocks the Light!

No wonder we sometimes doubt that the Light even exists. (Such doubts are classic ego consciousness, by the way.)

To be sure, we all struggle with our egos. But Kabbalah, being a technology and not a religion, tells us that the problem with ego is not that it's morally wrong or sinful; it's simply shoddy technology. Ego convinces you that self-centered, "me-first" insensitivity is an effective business model, when in fact the opposite is true.

But wait a minute, you might be saying. Aren't those egotistical blowhards we've all met—those guys who are so full of themselves and so thoroughly insensitive to others—the very ones who always manage to get ahead? The answer is that people like these might succeed for a while, but not permanently. And they certainly don't enjoy true prosperity.

But since we are consumed by ego so much of the time, we do need to work around it. We need to devise a strategy that puts ego to good use, like a relative working for your firm who needs to be assigned a task that will keep him out of trouble. (He may be more of a problem than an asset, but you can't fire him!)

So let's turn ego into a power for good; let's put this negative force to work for us. Ego is a dangerous tool because it can ruin as well as drive us—but if we don't let it control us, it can spur us on to great achievements.

In the 1970s, auto executive Lee Iacocca was thrown out of Ford Motor Company following a bitter fight with management. Shortly thereafter, Iacocca was approached for the job of president of Chrysler, Ford's perennial rival and a company that had fallen on hard times. "It's too far gone," Iacocca told his wife. "I can't do it."

"Mr. Ford will certainly be happy to hear that," his wife replied.

And that's all it took.

Lee Iacocca went on to take the reins at Chrysler, effecting one of the most dramatic turnarounds in U.S. corporate history. Ego was the driving force at Chrysler, but what truly cemented Iacocca's success was the fact that his efforts transcended ego. Chrysler became a cause for him, not a job. And because the goal was bigger than his personal agenda, he rallied thousands of people to create miracles in a town that was badly in need of them.

What Lee Iacocca tapped into—and what you need in your life—is a powerful tool called higher purpose.

IT'S NOT ABOUT ME

Scientists say in that our natural state, we use about 4% of our brain. Such is the state of our domination by the Competitor. But it need not be so.

Join the resistance! Fight the program! When we rise above ego nature, we gain access to the other 96% of the brain—the 96% from which the great business ideas come from, and from which inspired information and messages from the universe seem to appear like bolts from the blue. The *blue* is just another term for the unused 96% of the brain.

Can you use big new ideas in your business rather than small old ones? Can you, like the technician at 3M's research laboratories, try to develop a strong adhesive but fail, and instead it becomes an adhesive that sticks to objects but can easily be lifted off? And can you then say, "Hey, let's use this glue on yellow pieces of paper and call them 'post-it notes'"?

As a charter member of the resistance movement, resolve that your business will be about more than just your ego —that it will instead have a higher purpose. Your business can be about providing an environment that nurtures employees or securing a stellar education for your kids. Or it can be about bringing joy to people by means of a cool new product. It may even be an engine of growth for your community. It can be about any number of things—but it can't just be about you.

Chances are you have a Sony thingamajig or two in your house. Sony was born in the rubble of Japan's defeat in World War II, when the country's image lay in ruins along with its economy. Sony's higher purpose was to give people around the world a reason to like Japan again. And because it was imbued with a higher purpose, Sony plugged into Light consciousness. That consciousness filtered down the hierarchy to every desk and every corner of the company—and, not surprisingly, Sony became a global powerhouse.

When you're in business, you need to get Light into your corner. If your business is nothing more than a stage for the drama of your emotions and reactions, you may achieve temporary success, but it won't last. And you can be sure that it won't bring you true prosperity.

Ego is simply not a sustainable growth engine.

And the amazing thing is that when your business is not about you, it suddenly becomes a lot more fun!

ENJOY THE PROCESS

The Light has a request: It asks that you enjoy the process. Connecting to the Light is like taking part in a movie that is guaranteed to have a happy ending. Even as the storms rage and the bad guys attack, you play your part, but inside you're not worried. That's because you know you're going to end up defeating the villains and walking into the sunset with Julia Roberts or Brad Pitt on your arm.

As boss, you know the key: When the challenges arise, you're responsible. You know that you are the cause, not the effect. So the first time trouble raises its head, you don't rush headlong into victim consciousness. Indeed, it never even enters your mind to say, "The universe is punishing me!" Instead, you embrace your problems. You see them as opportunities to achieve greatness by confronting the Competitor and overcoming the challenge that faces you.

Light consciousness lets you enjoy the process. Who cares if there's a setback at this particular moment in time? You see the Big Picture, and it looks good.

You don't have to get overly excited when things are going well or, conversely, tumble into depression when they aren't. Enjoy yourself, and the universe will open up. Set goals that keep you excited, and don't hesitate to change them along the way. Recognize that while the Competitor put a system in place to bring us down, that force is also an opportunity to push back up and become the cause of our own movement forward.

In Light consciousness, we seek happiness from a position of happiness, not from the need to get happy. In other words, you're not filling an empty space; you're already complete, and your work is an expression of that completeness.

There's only one investment we need to make, and only one thing we need to sacrifice—and that is our ego. But don't worry; the ego is just an illusion anyway.

Stress Is A Surfboard

Stress is the collision between what you are and what you could be; it's a wave that rolls through your life. But if you're going to be the cause rather than the effect, you won't confront that wave by saying, "I can't handle it." Instead you'll say, "Hey, dude, this is a gnarly one—but I'm going to ride it."

When you hop a wave and ride it, you're harnessing the energy of that wave and using it to soar to new heights.

According to Kabbalah, there is a system for the Light and the container for the Light. Who are we? We're containers for the Light. It is the Light within us that sustains us and allows us to function. But there is yet another Light in addition to our inner Light, and Kabbalah calls it Surrounding Light. This represents our potential. All the abundance that lies out there waiting for us, all the money, the deals, the ideas, the family barbecues, the true fulfillment beyond anything we can conceive—exists now in a state of potential.

And that's where stress comes in. The tension between inner Light and Surrounding Light—between potential and actuality—is stress.

This is good news, though, because it means that stress, in essence, is Light. We may proclaim that stress kills, but in reality it is not stress that kills; it is our reaction to it. Sometimes we react to the Light by finding various ways of shutting it out. But when we shut off the Light, we are in fact killing ourselves - so the idea is not to turn stress away, but to let it in.

And to use it for one heck of a ride!

STRESS IS LIGHT!

The areas where we have stress are very special ones because they highlight the dark places in our lives— places that the stress has illuminated for us as though it were a flashlight, showing us where we need to direct our attention. These are the places Light has been blocked by our negative actions. Egocentric, self-centered behavior has created these patches of darkness, providing a road map for the Light. Like a spiritual detergent, Light washes through us to get at those hard-to-reach stains.

Stress, then, is not just a surfboard to ride; it's also an agent of cleansing. Like all negative conditions, which are there only to teach us, we must embrace stress. At the end of a washing machine cycle, the shirt is clean. If we embrace stress wholeheartedly, not only will stress not have an adverse effect, it will have an amazing effect. It will empower us to achieve greater fulfillment and to realize our full potential, affording us access to more ideas, more money, and more true prosperity.

A classic kabbalistic story is told that reveals how stress acts as a flashlight, finding the darkness for us. The story concerns a man whose beloved child suddenly falls ill. As time goes on, the child gets sicker and sicker, until finally the doctor tells the man that no hope remains; nothing can be done to save the child. Distraught, the man takes his sick child and races to his local kabbalist, imploring him that he is the child's one last hope. The kabbalist goes to his chambers and meditates, connects to the different Light through kabbalistic prayer, and finally comes up with an idea. "Go into town," he tells his assistant, "and gather up ten thieves. Get ten of the most villainous men you can find—men who are truly skilled at their wicked craft—and bring them to me."

Although confused, the loyal assistant runs to town, gathers the ten most malevolent people he can find, and brings them to the kabbalist for prayer. A half hour later, there is a knock at the door. It is the man whose child was dying, but his face is now radiant with joy. "My child is breathing easily," the man says. "His color is back. He's going to be all right!"

After the grateful man departs, the assistant turns to the kabbalist and says, "You could have had anyone meditate with you. You could have gathered the most enlightened and most righteous beings to pray for this boy. Surely they could have done more than the scoundrels you asked me to seek out!" The kabbalist looks at his assistant and gently responds, "When I saw that the Gates of Heaven were locked for this young boy, I knew that there was nothing I could do. But then a thought came to me, and it was then that I had you bring a band of thieves to help me. I realized that good thieves know all about breaking and entering. So they picked the locks! These criminals broke into the Gates of Heaven, and that is the only way my prayers were able to make their way into the heavenly sanctuary."

As you might have guessed, the thieves of this ancient legend represent our negative and egocentric traits. When we identify and work to transform our self-centered qualities and crooked characteristics, the key turns and the gates unlock. Blessings and good fortune then rain down upon us. Our negative traits are the key!

If we want to know what's holding us back, we must search for the darkness, because only through the darkness will you find the light. And that is what stress does: It finds the darkness, and right behind it, we find the Light.

Without stress, we couldn't bring the Surrounding Light into our lives. Without stress, we reach the natural limits of complacency; we hit the wall that keeps our company from moving to the next level—the wall that keeps us from achieving the greatness we're meant to attain. For this reason, far from being an annoyance and something to avoid, stress is a gift to seek!

The first thing I ask people when they tell me they're stuck is, Are you avoiding stress? When it comes, do you duck? Are you taking something to escape it—food, or sex, or drugs—just to get along?

Stress is a gift, but it often comes with its debilitating twin - something that can also be a gift. And that is . . .

FEAR.

Fear. Can You Take The Heat?

Once, two patients in a mental institution decided to plot their escape. In preparation for this, they divided up the necessary tasks. One man would gather the provisions; the other would investigate the wall surrounding the building and would then devise a plan. If the wall is lower than six feet, the first patient said to his partner, we'll jump it. If it's higher, we'll tunnel underneath.

At midnight, the first man stole into the kitchen, grabbed some food, and went to meet the second man. But when he arrived, he was in for a surprise. His partner was sitting there weeping. "We're never going to get out," the distraught patient said.

"Why?" the first man asked.

"There's no wall," the patient responded.

Fear is just such a wall in our minds. It doesn't really exist; it's simply there to show us there is something that needs to be fixed. Both fear and stress are forces that are given to us to help us move forward. But most of the time they have the opposite effect: They keep us stuck in the same place, or they take us backward.

FALSE EVIDENCE APPEARING REAL

Fear is an illusion, which is precisely why we say that the word fear stands for **F**alse **E**vidence **A**ppearing **R**eal. A study conducted by the University of Pennsylvania recently found that 40% of our worries never materialize. The study further revealed that 30% of our worries deal with the past, and nothing can be done about them. Another 12% were found to be directed toward other people's business, and nothing can be done about them. Another 10% were spent on imagined illnesses. Only 8% of worries were found to be justified.

Fear operates much the way stress does in your life: It pinpoints exactly what you need to focus on.

But getting back to prosperity, which is why we're here, let us ask this: Are you afraid of success? Kabbalistically, fear of success is really inverted ego, the inversion of a fear of failure. It is a way of saying, "If I never have to succeed, I never have to fail."

Yet stress and fear are your wisest business advisers, so don't turn away from them; instead, embrace them. I think of stress and fear as a steam bath. What happens in a steam bath? You sit down, and suddenly you feel as though there's no air to breathe. The hot steam fills the room and envelopes you, and your first impulse is to try to escape. But if you just sit with it, the steam cleanses you and eventually clears, and you emerge from the bath a new person.

Fear and stress are a steam room conveniently located right inside your business. So embrace the steam and embrace the heat. Just sit down and let them do their work.

The secret of the universe is that it's never a contest between you and your obstacles, or between you and your fears; it's about you and God. It's about you and the Light you will reveal, the prosperity you will enjoy and share. The obstacles only involve how you will reveal the Light. You can be slowed by fear and stress, or you can recognize that they are there to help you move forward.

And, as boss in your life, it is up to *you* to move forward; no one else is going to do the work for you. Research has shown that 90% of businesses fail in their first year of operation. One reason for this lies in **F**alse **E**vidence **A**ppearing **R**eal. Trouble, you say? Uh-oh—we'd better bail! In point of fact, there is no financial organization on earth—no office or workplace in the world—that is free of tensions and anxieties. When you experience stress with someone, it's a signal to be responsible and take care of that problem now. It is a message to *do* something, and that message will only grow stronger the longer you put it off. Fear gets worse when you avoid dealing with it.

Suppose you are in a desert and you have two guides. You don't want to flee from them or ignore their advice, do you? In much the same way, stress and fear are your guides - and though your first impulse may well be to get rid of them, you must guard against that impulse.

Without the kabbalistic tools and strategies we are outlining in this book, you will want to destroy your guides, or at best find ways simply to cope with them. But with the tools of Kabbalah, you will be able to embrace your guides, and in so doing allow them to lead you out of the desert and into the oasis known as true prosperity.

All you need is . . .

CERTAINTY

Okay, so you're becoming the cause, not the effect, on the path to wealth and prosperity.

You've set goals, knowing that goals are not the goals but just the net that helps you get a great shot. You've realized that building your business on a foundation of egocentric impulses is a defective business model, and you've recognized that the secret of sustained growth is higher purpose. You know that stress is a surfboard to ride, that fear is an illusion to be exposed, and that both are tools to show you where work needs to be done—work that will transform your nature and allow you to connect with the 99% realm.

The bedrock for all this activity is certainty. You will be successful when you have it, and you won't be when you don't. If you are not certain that you can turn fear and stress into your allies—if you don't have absolute certainty that you deserve prosperity and merit more wealth than you know what to do with—then the universe will make sure you don't have it.

Certainty is the power cord for every technology in this book. Without certainty, this book is nothing more than a bunch of Black & Decker power tools lying around with no electrical outlet to plug them in. In the end, you're not going be able to build a thing with them.

If your attitude is, "Well, nothing's worked for me so far, and these kabbalistic tools probably won't either, but what the heck, I'll give them a try," kindly stop wasting your time, and deposit this book in the nearest trash bin.

Certainty is something we discover. It's not some kind of positive thinking we spread over our doubts like raspberry jelly. And this is because . . .

Certainty Is Light Consciousness

Certainty is just plain knowing. The rational mind is close-ly allied with the Competitor, and he likes to have you think about it. And *think about it*. And think about it.

With certainty, you no longer stumble through chaos hoping things will turn out all right—hoping the market will turn, or that people will suddenly develop a fondness for green shorts just because they happen to be what you're selling.

When you trust the Light, you are sharing; your business has a higher purpose than your personal agenda, and you have certainty.

No amount of genius—no MBAs or PhDs from Harvard, not even being a good person—will guarantee you true prosperity as much as certainty.

When you have certainty, you're no longer at the mercy of every little thing that happens. You're in the driver's seat, and from that vantage point, you can manage the single most vital resource you have been given. And that is your . . .

TIME

What is time, exactly?

That's a good question.

A BRIEF KABBALISTIC HISTORY OF TIME

Scientists struggle with time. They're still not sure what it is.

But Kabbalah tells us that time was given to us by none other than our Competitor.

Question: Why would this Opponent, the Ultimate Competitor in the business of our life, create such a strange thing as time?

Answer: Time exists for the sole purpose of allowing us free will so that we can fulfill our destinies and be the cause in our own lives—so that we can become like God and Creator in our own universe and thereby earn the Light.

To be sure, that's a lot to take in—and since it is highly unlikely that anyone has ever explained time to you in quite this way, I'll give it to you again: Time is a gift. It allows us to exercise our free will. Free will gives us the opportunity to become the cause—the boss in the business of life—and allows us to earn our own fulfillment rather than having Bread of Shame.

But how does time allow us to exercise our free will? Let's take a closer look.

THE GAP BETWEEN CAUSE AND EFFECT

According to Kabbalah, the gap between cause and effect is called time, and that gap allows us freedom of choice. Because if cause and effect were instantly linked—if every time you hurt someone, they instantly hurt you back—you would quickly learn never to do anything wrong. It would be stupid! You would do something wrong, and then *boom*—you would feel the consequences. In such an instant-feedback universe, who wouldn't be a righteous, unselfish, caring person?

But it would all be too easy, because it would take away free will.

So time enters the equation, and now things become much more mysterious, because now you can't see the cause and effect. You might even come to doubt the existence of cause and effect altogether.

FICTION

The great dramatist Oscar Wilde once defined fiction this way: It's where the good are rewarded and the bad are punished. Such cynicism is possible only when the gap between cause and effect blinds you to its predictability, and only when it appears as though evil people get away with nefarious deeds while good people are left to suffer. Perhaps someone lied and stole your money, or a business skipped town without paying you—and yet they both seem to be prospering, Meanwhile, remember that sweet woman who worked so hard at the office and was so caring to all her coworkers? She got fired!

One percent consciousness might see these examples as proof that there is no cause and effect—that there is no justice to be found. But that's because 1% consciousness blinds you to the role that time plays in separating cause and effect.

When you connect to Light consciousness, the secrets are revealed. No one gets away with anything, because external reality is an illusion. Every action comes back at you, it is true—but it's even more immediate than that. Every action really doesn't go anywhere to begin with. The negativity built up by selfish and egocentric behavior accumulates and forms one curtain after another, blocking you from the Light.

So time allows us the freedom to choose. We can choose the 1% path or the 99% path. We can be the Light, or we can venture down a road filled with victim conscious-ness, chaos, and unfulfilled desires—a road that leads to a realm in which nothing ever persists. But if we choose the Light, the path leads to everything we need. Sure we'll have our ups and downs, but we'll enjoy the thrill of accomplishment as we do so.

THE WOMAN IN THE DREAM

Once, there was a man so wise that even at an early age he had become an eminent spiritual teacher. One night the man had a dream in which an older woman came to him urgently seeking help with her children, and his assistance was so vital to her that it appeared she would hurt herself if he couldn't offer his aid. The man woke up deeply affected by the dream, and throughout that day he remained alert, knowing full well that the dream had been important—that an elderly woman was in urgent need of his help. So while the woman didn't come the first day or the second, the man remained alert for several weeks. But as time went on, he began to forget. He remembered that a woman was coming to him, but he forgot why. Then he remembered that he'd had a dream, but he couldn't remember what the dream had been about. Then he forgot the dream altogether.

Many years passed. The man was in his 60s when one night, at 3 A.M., there was a knock on his door. His wife answered. At the door was an elderly woman who said that she had an urgent question for the teacher. His wife woke him right away, but the teacher, who was tired after a long day, asked if she could come back in the morning. Then suddenly he remembered his dream and raced downstairs. The woman was gone. "Did she mention something about her children?" he asked, and his wife nodded. It was then that the teacher realized that this was the woman from his dream long ago—so he bolted from the house, searching frantically for her. When he finally found the old woman, she had already tried to kill herself but was still alive, and he was able to restore her to health.

Because of the time lag, the teacher didn't connect his dream to the old woman's arrival at his door. Because of the disconnect between cause and effect, the woman had to suffer—but the teacher finally made the connection, so her life was saved.

We get clues along the way; we get messages from the universe about the direction we should take. Sometimes the information may appear random, but if we can make the connections, it can change everything. We have the power to connect information, and by doing so we can shrink cause and effect.

What I'm saying is that we have the power to remove time from our existence!

Time Is A Rubber Band

Let's say you have a five-year plan for your business. You start up, you get your loans, you build the business, you pay back the loans, and you start making money—all in five years. Very nice. But do you really want to wait five years?

What if you could shrink five years into one year? Or one month? With the tools of Kabbalah, you have just that power. You could have everything you're going to make in the next 15 years right now. You never knew you had the power to shrink time, but you do. Time is elastic when you plug into Light consciousness.

When you have certainty and just **know** that things will happen—when you harness the ego that drives us rather than the ego that pulls us down—you can shorten time and eliminate the gap between cause and effect. And it is then that time will work for you.

When time works for you, you can not only shorten the time between cause and effect—one stretch of the rubber band—but also lengthen the time you have to achieve your priorities—the other stretch of the rubber band.

Some live 70 years like one day.
Some live one day like 70 years.

—King David

Money comes and money goes. You can always make more, but when time slips away, it's never coming back again.

Kabbalah tells us that time is our most precious non renewable natural resource. So you need to ask yourself the following questions:

Are you being productive with your time, or are you just busy?

Are you defining priorities and sticking to them like Crazy Glue? Or are you just doing . . . whatever?

If we don't appreciate the time we are given, our time will not have the Light.

That is the truth about time. When our time doesn't have the Light, we play right into the Competitor's hands. Without the Light, we find that we continually end up in the wrong place at the wrong time and make "brilliant" decisions we later regret.

Take the time to establish your priorities and treat your time as if it were a precious jewel, and an amazing thing will happen: The Light will guide you. Even if your priority proves wrong, the Light will shift your focus to the right thing. By simply making the effort to establish priorities, you will find yourself in the right place at the right time doing precisely the right thing. **Be the cause of time, not the effect of it.**

USE TIME: DON'T LET TIME USE YOU

There is so much more you could do every day! The Bible tells us that King David was quite an efficient manager of his time. He certainly accomplished a great deal in his illustrious career. It was he who observed that time is malleable—that it bends differently for each person depending on their consciousness.

The Internet bubble may well have burst, but it taught us a profound lesson. Employees at high-tech companies were secretaries one day and millionaires the next. The lesson here is that time is an illusion and that abundance can happen instantly—and when the Light is in your corner, you don't have to wait years for wealth to show up.

We don't want our abundance when we're 90; we want it now. And we can have it as long as we act like the Light —as long as we are the cause and not the effect in our lives, as long as we conduct ourselves with certainty.

Time is money, time is Light, and time is in our control —so we can become beings of abundance and true prosperity and have everything we want right now!

FILL YOUR JAR WITH ROCKS

Once a master called his students together and showed them a large clay jar. "Help me fill this jar with rocks," he asked. So the students gathered up nearby rocks and filled the jar until not one more rock could fit.

"Is the jar filled now?" the master asked.

The students all replied yes. But the master picked up some pebbles and asked, "Do you think we can fit any of these inside?"

So the students began filling the jar with pebbles, and though just a minute earlier they had considered the jar full, they were amazed at how many pebbles could fit inside the spaces between the rocks. The jar took hundreds of pebbles, and then finally no more could fit.

"Is the jar full now?" the master asked, and again the students responded yes.

And the master replied, "Very well, but perhaps some sand could fit inside," and he started pouring sand into the jar. Once again the students were amazed at how much space there was for sand between the pebbles. Finally, every last inch of the jar was full.

"This is a lesson," the master resumed. "If we had started by putting in the sand, we would never have been able to put in the pebbles. If we had started by putting in the pebbles, we would have never have been able to put in the big rocks. This jar is like the vessel of your own souls. You need to fill your souls with the big things first. When you do that, you'll be surprised at how much space is left for everything else."

Focus on what's important, and not only will you accomplish those things, but somehow everything else on your list will get done as well. But if you focus on the small things, you'll never get to the big ones.

Waste your time on things that aren't priorities, and you won't get to the priorities. Your time will simply vanish.

Fill your jar with rocks first, and there will be room for sand and pebbles too.

Here's an exercise: Write down your priorities for the week, the month, and the year. Then number them. Be honest and carve out the priorities that will get your business and your life where you want them to go. Then use that list like holy scripture. Go back to it repeatedly, and make sure you're focusing on the direction of your priorities: one-two-three-four-five.

Priorities demonstrate the power of focus.

Whatever we focus on is what will materialize in our lives.

You are the boss in the business of your life. Your focus is your power. Don't waste that power! If you focus on small things, small things will show up in your life.

When you set your priorities, bear in mind that those priorities—like everything else in your life—must have a higher purpose. You are connecting to Light consciousness, not to ordinary, everyday, reactive, 1% consciousness. You are the Light, not the container, so your priorities must have other people in the equation. Make it your priority that humanity will be served by your actions, and that as a citizen of the world, you will take steps to help erase some of the pain and suffering that blanket the planet.

Alternatively, your priority could simply be to provide a better life for your wife, lover, partner, kids, or parents—if in fact that priority is *truly* about them. Just make sure it isn't just about **you**, because that will guarantee that **you** will reap no benefit.

If this sounds like a paradox, welcome to the universe! **The rules are set up so that you serve yourself by serving others, even if you have to drag your ego to the party kicking and screaming.** Conversely, you are your own worst enemy when you are the only factor in the equation.

So as long as the priorities you set have the purpose of using money to benefit others, there will be Light in your time.

When you involve the Light by being unselfish, you will be successful. And your prosperity won't be here today and gone tomorrow; instead, it will last through time.

Did I say time? That reminds me. Stop being . . .

A FIREFIGHTER!

I'll repeat that: Stop being a firefighter.

We all seem to spend our time putting out fires. **We are an emergency assistance crew in our own lives, on call 24 hours a day.** But by the time we finish our daily rounds, we discover that there's no time left over for anything important. The firefighting has consumed us.

Of course, the Competitor is delighted to hear this. In fact, the Competitor is the very one who sets these fires to begin with. Emergency over here—whoops! There's one over there, too. Uh-oh—there's a crisis on the third floor. Yikes, that supplier is going nuts!

The Competitor loves to watch us as we continue in our hot pursuit, extinguishing one fire after another and, in so doing, extinguishing our ability to be fulfilled— because as firefighters, our lives can only become one vast game of postponement. We tell ourselves that once we have put all the fires out, we will finally have enough time left over to think about abundance, joy, and our relation- ships—the true stuff of prosperity. But of course, the fires never end.

Here, then, is a mantra: **I am a bigger vessel than a fire- fighter.** (Of course I mean this as a metaphor; I have nothing but admiration for professional firefighters!) This fire, that fire; each one seems to be the crisis of crises —but this is an illusion. When I have certainty that my life is not about fires, those fires will become the rare exception rather than the rule.

When you have power and certainty, it's almost as if the fires give up. **This fire is called on account of lack of interest.**

Soon the fires become the background rather than the foreground—annoyances and not tragedies—and take up less and less of your time. Instead of a day, how about an hour?

What, then, is the problem with being the fireman of your life? It causes you to lose appreciation of time. And Light comes only when we focus and appreciate the time that is given to us.

When we are the effect of time, we fall into the illusion of it. Time wasted creates a space in which negativity can enter. But inject certainty, sharing, and productivity into your time, and get ready for amazing things to happen.

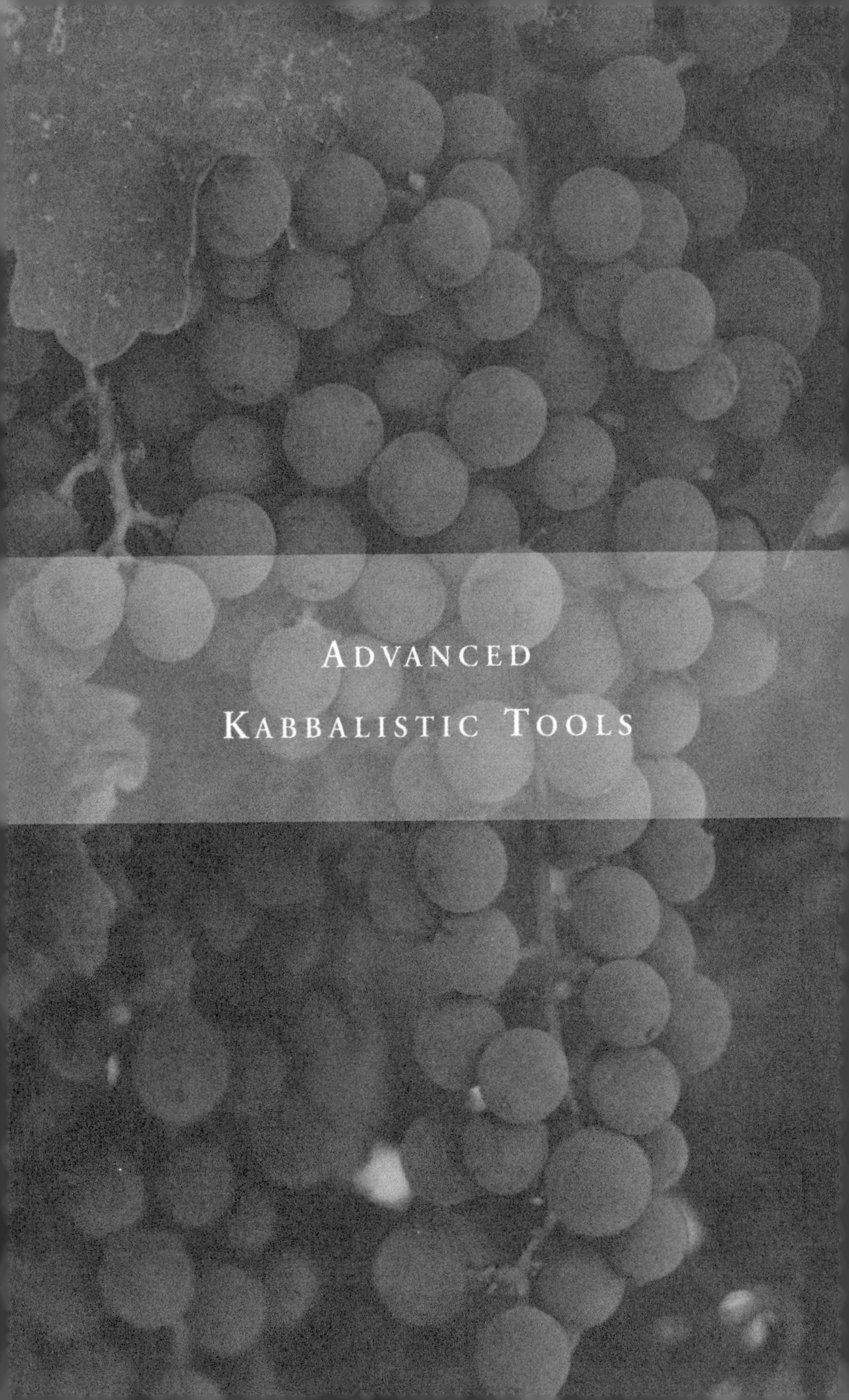

Advanced Kabbalistic Tools

TITHING

Kabbalists believe that if you want to make money, it's a good idea to start by knowing what it is. So let's review what we do know. Is money that green stuff with presidents printed on it? No. Is money a series of numbers printed by some computer on a bank statement? No. Is money a bunch of gold bars buried in a vault? No.

As we've learned, money isn't anything physical at all. Money is **energy!** And understanding that money is energy—that money is Light—is the basis of the kabbalistic technology of tithing.

Most religions speak of tithing and recommend it as a tool of sharing. The Bible itself states that we should give

10% of our income to charity through tithing. But why is tithing so important, and why 10%? Is tithing a necessary annoyance? An **unnecessary** annoyance? Or is it a tool of abundance and protection?

THE 10% SOLUTION

Kabbalah tells us that tithing 10% is built into the fabric of the universe itself. Again, it is a matter of science, not religion.

Amazingly, the most cutting-edge thinkers of modern Superstring Theory and the most ancient-edge thinkers of Kabbalah both agree on the same magical number. The universe has ten dimensions—ten different energy levels.

Saying that the universe has ten dimensions is another way of saying that there are ten versions of you. One version is the you that's here right now—the one to whom the telephone company sends its bills. And then there are all the potential you's that become possible as you attain higher levels of fulfillment and deeper levels of prosperity. The universe is like an elevator—you can choose whichever floor you want to be on. But there's a catch: The only way we're allowed to get on that elevator is if we clean up our 1% existence.

The tenth level is the 1% realm, the world we live in—and according to Kabbalah, no one is either strong enough or spiritual enough to have dominion over this realm. It is here that we fall into the traps of the Competitor in that each of us has ego as well as anger, and each of us carries within us the residue of the hurt we've done to others—the residue of being the effect rather than the cause. All this needs to be cleaned up.

Tithing 10% is the way to cleanse the 1% realm.
Tithing cleanses the tenth dimension, and once we've
taken care of that, we're allowed to ride that elevator up
to any dimension we choose.

IF WE DON'T GIVE, WE CAN'T GET MORE

Tithing is the ultimate paradox of the universe, because it means that the more you want to get, the more you have to give. The 10% we give cleanses the remaining 90%. It's like having ten oranges and one goes rotten; you need to get rid of the rotten one or risk spoiling all the rest. The 10% tithe erases guilt and obliterates obstacles to true prosperity.

So here's a quick answer to the question you're now asking yourself: to tithe or not to tithe?

The answer is, there is really no good alternative.

I told you this wouldn't take long!

If you keep the 10%, the Competitor now has access to your life. That money you've clung to creates a tiny hole —a crevice that the Competitor can use to gain entry into you life. Through that 10% hole, the Competitor can help himself to anything and everything he wants, slowly draining you of your assets bit by bit, be those assets spiritual or monetary. Tithing is the way to "buy out" your Competitor so that he no longer has any say in how you run your business—or your life! Tithing is a buy-out clause; either you exercise it or you don't. But as Don Vito Corleone might have said, it's an offer you can't refuse—because somewhere along the line, the universe will take 10% anyway. It may be a bad business deal, or a year when for no good reason you make less money than you did the year before—but somehow, somewhere, the system will make sure that 10% is taken. So the only question that remains is, will you do it proactively or reactively?

And don't think that it is money you have to tithe. You can also tithe your time. Time, like money, is energy, and when we make a gift of our time by taking action to help others, it will cleanse the 10% equally well.

IN MONEY WE TRUST?

In God we trust. That's what's written on that nice, crisp dollar bill you're holding, and it couldn't be clearer. What kabbalists and your dollar bill are both trying to tell you is that security does not reside in money; instead, it resides purely in the Light. There is no security in the 1% realm, no matter how many truckloads of cash you might have. Ask the billionaire who can't find a cure for his child's fatal illness. Or weigh the power your checkbook holds against terrorist attacks and tsunamis.

We still think of money as security, and sometimes it seems as if no amount of evidence to the contrary can change our minds. It's as though we've been backing a horse that has lost 10,000 straight races, but we're ready to bet on him one more time—because we're convinced that this time he's coming in. What's worse, if I think that money is the basis for my security, I can't give my money away. I can't be generous, for I don't feel I have enough to give. John and Phyllis over there, they're rich, we might say. They can afford to give it away. They can tithe; they can share. If I had their money, I could tithe too. But I can't. Sorry!

Money is energy, and to get more, we have to share. Something that isn't shared doesn't stick around forever. But something shared gets replenished; it's a law of the universe. If two people are in a relationship and there is no true sharing, the relationship cannot last.

If there's anything we want to keep, we need to keep the energy flowing. Sharing must be part of it. And this holds true even of money.

So if you're just starting out and can give only 5%, that's okay—but remember, tithing is science. It's as if one of the ten dimensions were being given away to protect the other nine. That 90% can then grow to be 9000%. Through tithing, we achieve true prosperity.

But tithing must be done with the right consciousness.

THE CAKE TASTES DIFFERENT!

Imagine two professional chefs. Each takes exactly the same ingredients and proceeds to bake a cake. When they're finished, we sample the results: first Cake A, and then Cake B.

Voilà! Cake B tastes better than Cake A.

But how can that be? Both cakes were baked by experienced chefs using the exact same recipe and the exact same ingredients. So how can one cake taste better than other?

The answer is that Cake B had a special ingredient called consciousness. Chef B simply breathed positive energy into the cake, and that made a difference in terms of its taste. (Did you ever see the movie *Chocolat*? If not, I highly recommend it.)

The lesson of the cakes is that ultimately the universe is not physical. (This is a big lesson for a cake, but according to Kabbalah, wisdom shows up in unexpected places.) The universe is consciousness—so the consciousness, the thoughts, and the mind-set with which you perform an action will profoundly affect the results.

When you give tithing with the right consciousness, you will receive not only for yourself but for your family as well. And the right consciousness means tithing willingly and joyfully—not because you have to or because your rabbi or priest told you to, but because you're thrilled to do something that will provide an antidote to the negativity in your life, something that will give you a rocket boost to abundance.

So how do you measure the consciousness with which you give? First, it's vital to be honest with yourself about where you stand. The Competitor lives in the grey areas; he likes it when you're being a little good and a little bad. So bring as much clarity to this process as you can. Ask yourself continually: What kind of giver am I?

Here are the levels of giving consciousness, from the lowest to the highest. Where do you stand?

THE SCALE OF SHARING

Level One: THE BEGRUDGING GIVER.
I don't really want to give, and when I do, I give grudgingly.

Level Two: THE UNDER-GIVER.
I give a lot less than I can afford and a lot less than I should, but I'm happy to make at least some contribution.

Level Three: REACTIVE SHARING.
Someone asks me for a favor or someone close to me needs help, so I agree.

Level Four: PROACTIVE SHARING.
I don't need to be asked. I can see when somebody needs assistance, and I take the initiative to offer it.

Level Five: UNCOMFORTABLE SHARING.
This is sharing outside the comfort zone. (In Kabbalah, know that any time you are outside the comfort zone, you are in the right place!) You may never have given to this person before, or it may be more than you feel comfortable giving, but you go ahead anyway.

Level Six: SHARING WITHOUT RECOGNITION.
This is anonymous sharing. You know where the money is going, but the person or organization receiving it doesn't know who the giver is. This is nonego sharing and is ranked very high!

Level Seven: SHARING WITHOUT AGENDA.
You don't know where the money is going, *and* the receiver doesn't know where it came from. Your tithing is arranged through a third party such as a family member or a trusted friend. This is truly high-level sharing,

Level Eight: PROACTIVE ACTION SHARING.
Here, you cut off someone's pain and suffering before it even happens. You anticipate that a negative situation may befall them, and you share with them so as to avoid the situation rather than waiting until they're in trouble before you help. This is a tremendous level of sharing.

Level Nine: GLOBAL-SCALE SHARING.
You give to a place or to an organization that not only takes care of things on a small scale, but also attempts to change the world. This is world-class tithing—tithing that can effect changes on a global scale. Our goal at The Kabbalah Centre is to be an organization that addresses the needs of humanity on that scale, and we invite you to look for other such organizations.

Level Ten: ALL OF THE ABOVE.
These are the various levels of sharing. Always ask your-self where you stand on the scale, because clarity and truth are the Competitor's most bitter enemies. And here's an amazing tip: You don't have to wait until you give before you start earning the protection of tithing.

GAIN CONTROL TODAY

You can build your tithing right into your financial plan. It's very simple.

Say you want to earn a million dollars over the coming year. (Why not aim high?) Set your plans, and tune your consciousness to make $1.1 million. That is, build the 10% tithing into your anticipated income.

This way, you're planning your sharing before you even make the money. You want to make $1.1 million so that you can keep $1 million and protect that $1 million by giving away 10%. Now, this is proactive sharing! You're gaining control of your money today. You're accessing the light of protection today from all the negativity out there that might be working its way through your finances and well-being.

Scientists recently found a black hole in the Milky Way that is estimated to be 30 million times the size of our sun! Bear in mind that there are black holes in your life as well—people who are jealous of you, gossip about you, and judge you. Although conventional wisdom may hold that words do no harm, Kabbalah knows that the jealousy, judgment, and envy of others can tangibly affect our well-being and cause us no end of sickness and pain. Tithing protects you from all of this.

I SHARE, THEREFORE I AM (PROTECTED)

Please remember that you are not tithing in order to become a good person; you are tithing in order to gain the practical benefit of protection from chaos. Giving 10% is a lot cheaper than turning your business over to the Competitor. You are the boss as long as you operate proactively. But the minute you are the effect - the minute you don't have protection - the Competitor will break into your office and rifle your files. He'll wreak havoc on your bottom line as well as on your peace of mind. He'll ignite fire after fire and have you running around like an overextended emergency worker to put them all out.

Protection is a kind of consciousness: The more I share, the more I get. Each and every act of sharing will add to my protection.

So . . .

Right now . . .

Before the doubts come in,

Before your mind says, "Oh, come on,"

Before time passes,

Before you forget,

Before you come up with ten reasons not to,

Before the Competitor puts you back to sleep . . .

Take action!

See where you stand on the scale of sharing, and resolve to do something immediately.

NOW

AHORA

MAINTENANT

THIS SECOND

And then see what abundance, power, and true prosperity flow into your life.

THE TRUE PROSPERITY
COMPANY

BUILDING A SPIRITUAL COMPANY

A truly prosperous company is a spiritual company—but when I say "spiritual," it has nothing to do with a particular doctrine, dogma, or sect.

A spiritual company is simply an organization that is built on the principle that **if you take care of people, the Light will take care of you.**

Not only do you want to apply kabbalistic tools for yourself, you want to inject them into your company. Whether your company has one employee or 50,000, you want to be part of a business that produces abundance - not just in the near term, but forever.

Most people need motivation; people simply get less done when they're not motivated. Thus, part of injecting abundance into a truly prosperous company involves keeping the engines of motivation humming. Whatever level you're on, someone should be motivating you. A person above you should be motivating you, and you should be motivating someone below you.

But let's cut to the chase. In a spiritual company, people look out for each other. The needs of others become essential to you, and when someone is down, you're there for them. And when you're down, someone will be there for you.

In a spiritual company, you don't function with your head stuck in a cubicle, isolated and looking out for Number You-Know-What. Other people are important. Do you know the name of the person who sweeps up at the end of the day? If not, do you know the name of the person in the next cubicle?

It's so basic, and yet so many of us don't live this way. If you take care of people, the Light will take care of you.

Now, this may not sound familiar to you given your experiences in the cutthroat world of business. It may be that caring for others is as alien to your workplace as speaking Latin. Perhaps if you tried to explain these principles to fellow employees, they would look at you as if you'd grown an extra head. But does that mean you shouldn't put these ideas into practice?

Of course not. If you care for people—if you motivate them, go out of your way to share with them, and focus on what is needed rather than on what is wanted—somehow, in some way, the energy will all come back to you. You may not be able to figure out how, because sometimes it won't make any sense at all - but it works.

Just be certain; just know. The laws of cause and effect will come to your aid, and all the good you do for others will be returned to you many times over.

Know that this will happen, but at the same time don't expect it. This is a subtle but important point. When we give to others, we will receive in return, but we should not expect it to come from that particular person. That's not how it works. Indeed, if you give to someone with an expectation of return from that person, it's not truly giving.

For a company to have an energy flow, just give unconditionally, even if you're the only one who knows about it.

Don't expect a return on your investment. Be a sharing being, not a receiving being. Do it, and just let it go.

And don't be distracted by the things that destroy a spiritual company.

THE ENEMIES

There are five enemies of a truly prosperous company. Eliminate them as if they were toxic gases seeping into your office from the ventilation equipment.

Enemy One: The Dictator

They say that absolute power corrupts absolutely. And when a boss rules a company with an iron hand - when he embraces a "my-way-or-the-highway" management philosophy, dictating your every action and allowing employees no room in which to breathe or contribute - he will indeed corrupt that company absolutely.

Enemy Two: "Do as I Say, Not as I Do" Management

"People don't follow you because you have a title. People follow you because of your courage." So spoke the leader of the rebels in the movie Braveheart. This also holds true in a business context, where it refers to executive integrity within an organization. Leadership comes with the responsibility to walk the walk, not just talk the talk.

Enemy Three: Ego Above, Ego Below

Ego kills organizations wherever it surfaces, from the top all the way to the bottom of the food chain. Indeed, it's actually worse on the bottom. If a CEO is egocentric, at least there may be some explanation for it; perhaps he has an enormous burden on his shoulders. But if an underling has ego, you have to ask why. If you're a junior employee and you let your ego interfere with the needs of the company, you have only a short period of time to change on your own, or the universe will provide a much more efficient program for your education. It's called "being out on the street with your hat in your hand."

Enemy Four: Uncertainty

This malaise floats through many office environments: Employees have one foot in their jobs and one foot out the door. That adds up to a lot of feet to stumble over! Your business can't function on all cylinders, with everyone working wholeheartedly toward a common goal, when all your employees are out weighing other jobs or pondering the age-old question, Should I stay or should I go?

Enemy Five: Unpredictable Anger

Anger is toxic and can bring a company to its knees. Some people think anger is colorful and effective, the sign of a driven and relentless leader. Wrong! Kabbalah teaches that anger is one of the most dangerous conditions for human beings, causing disease in your body and ravishing the health of your business.

So those are the five enemies. They are viruses that threaten the life of your organization, and you need to root them out.

And when you do, ask yourself this:

How do I raise the consciousness of my company and transform it into a truly prosperous organization? How do I really know who is a talent and who is not? How do

I establish loyalty so that people don't bail at the first sign of trouble? How can I gauge the true worth of my employees and make sure I don't underpay or overpay them?

The answer to each of these questions lies in . . .

THE BIG PICTURE

If an employee thinks first about the needs of the employer and the company, and thinks only second about himself, he'll always be guided to the right answers. If an employer thinks first about the company and the employees, and thinks only second about himself, he'll always be guided to the right information. He'll know he should keep Arlene, let Timothy go, and give Rolonda a promotion. It's just that clear.

Wherever it is that you focus, that is where your answers will come from. When you think of yourself first, you will always get the wrong information. When everyone thinks of the company first, the company will achieve more and more. It will keep moving and rising and providing abundance to all who work there.

There is an ancient Aramaic word that kabbalists sometimes use. The word is **lezulat**. And it means . . .

For another.

The word *lezulat* is not a charming little piece of spiritual history; it's a secret code that will lead us to prosperity. We live in the "me-first" paradigm, and our belief system states that we will achieve more if we think about ourselves. We're always looking out for Number You-Know-What.

Wrong!

Kabbalah teaches that if you think of others—if you struggle to find what's good for them—you yourself can have more.

Do you believe in what you're doing? Does it pass the test of *lezulat*? Does what you're selling bring more Light into the 1% world? If you're thinking of starting a new company, consider *lezulat*: Will the goods or services you are offering to the world give people access to the 99% world?

Lezulat.

The book *The 60-Second Manager* makes the following suggestion: While you're trying to sell somebody something, take 60 seconds to think about the other person. If you were the person buying, how would you feel? This process immediately injects sharing into the equation— and when that happens, every decision you make will be based on Light. When we focus only on ourselves, we'll often end up doing the wrong thing.

Life is full of questions and answers. When my only agenda is to advance myself, the flow of energy and information has stopped. At every step, others must be injected into the equation.

Now there's one other thing you want to do: You want to forget about what you want. And you want to . . .

LEAD

Everything in this book points to one fundamental responsibility: You need to be a leader, not a follower.

And the first thing to know is that "leader" is not a job description. It is a state of consciousness.

A leader is a leader wherever he or she falls on the totem pole, whether he is a CEO or a receptionist—in charge of thousands or responsible for one computer.

So what makes someone a leader?

A leader has . . .

Certainty

A leader doesn't waver. A leader acts rather than reacts. A leader knows what he or she must do and why it must be done, and then does it. A leader isn't put off by discomfort or run aground by opposition. A leader knows that doing what needs to be done provides ultimate comfort for the soul, no matter how uncomfortable it may be for the ego.

A leader doesn't say, "This isn't my job; someone else will do it."

A leader says, "If I don't do this, no one's going to do it."

When you're a leader, everything is your job. If it needs to get done, you will do it. You will gladly pick up that piece of paper on the floor of the copy room, knowing that a clean environment is a safe environment. The child you're asked to keep an eye on for a moment becomes your child for that moment.

If you own a business, everything inside those four walls is your concern, right? Well, you're the boss of your life now, so everything is your concern. You are connected to all things, and it's not someone else's world; it's yours. You don't wait for someone to tell you what needs to be done. You decide.

A leader says, "I am not just another person. It's up to me." And only by being a leader do we have access to Light and true fulfillment.

LEADERSHIP IS CONTAGIOUS

When you're a leader, you affect people simply by being who you are. Once two speakers were lined up to give back-to-back talks at a business conference. The first was a slick, seasoned, highly charismatic motivational speaker. When he delivered his talk, people laughed, cheered, and listened. "What a great speech," they commented afterward. Then the second speaker got up. He was not so charismatic, engaging, or funny—but when his speech was over, people said, "Okay, where do we begin?"

The first speaker inspired people to listen. The second speaker didn't; he just inspired people to do something, which is the mark of a true leader. It isn't the greatest expert or the best transmitter of information who makes a true leader. It's the person who, when he's finished, motivates people to do more.

The definition of a leader is one who inspires people to be more than they are. And if you're not inspiring others, sorry—you're doing something wrong. If you're sharing and they're not listening, there's also something missing from the equation. When you start a club and no one wants to join, you're not a leader. And unless you're a leader, you can't achieve true prosperity.

And by the way, being a leader is a full-time job.

THE CAMERA'S ALWAYS ON

There are no part-time leaders. There's no walking the talk 60% of the time and then taking a break and talking the talk the rest of the time. Nope; either you're connected to the Light and leading, or you're not.

A famous presidential candidate was once caught saying something embarrassing. "Geez," he said, "I didn't know the camera was on." Well, when you're running for President, the camera is *always* on. And when you're a leader, it's always on too. You can't be one way in public and another at home, when you think "no one is watching." Either you're walking the walk or you're not. Either you're inspiring people all the time, or you're not.

ONE HUNDRED BILLION FOLLOWERS

Scientists estimate that over the course of time, 100 billion human beings have come and gone from this earth. And the overwhelming majority of them have left behind nothing but a tombstone.

Why do so many people vanish without a trace? Why are the giants whose names are now icons, from Abraham, Moses, and Jesus to Einstein, and Mother Teresa, so few in number? Why do so few who take the trouble to be born and suffer fail to leave a single mark?

Because most people choose to be followers, not leaders.

It's as simple as that. If you hunger to make a difference on this planet—to have enough impact so that people actually remember you—you need to be a leader.

We all have within us the power to be different. Each of us has the power to be a leader. And now, with the tools of Kabbalah, we have a technology that can transform our lives and enrich the lives of others, be it in the office, on the street, or playing with our kids.

People come and go. Companies do as well. Few remain, and fewer still are remembered. Is that the way things will go with you, or will you choose to be different?

CHOOSE TO BE DIFFERENT. BE TRUE TO YOURSELF

You've made mistakes. In fact, it's probably fair to say that you've messed up at times. I'm sure there are things you don't even want to remember—things you're not proud of having done, and things you hope they don't bring up when *60 Minutes* does a profile on you.

But that's great!

What do you become when you've made mistakes? You become an inspiration.

If I've gone bankrupt and have then gone on to rebuild my business from scratch, I can inspire someone else who has had to declare bankruptcy. If I've had problems as a parent or have neglected my body or my health, I can serve as an inspiration to all who might be grappling with just those issues.

When you can say, "I've been there," you're an inspiration, not a theoretician. People will listen, and you can use your experience to make a difference. And when you use all of your experience—both the good and the bad, the wonderful achievements and the idiotic mistakes,—with no residue of guilt about anything you've done, you're a leader.

You can always choose to be different. You can always choose not to be one of the 100 billion. Christopher

Reeve could have chosen to end it all, and no one would have faulted him. But he chose to take a different path, turning injury into inspiration. He was proactive, and even though he could barely move, he moved everybody else. He went . . .

FROM EFFECT TO CAUSE

Start being a leader. How do you do that? You do it by doing it.

At every moment, begin initiating. Turn cause and effect on its head.

Let's say you're at a job interview. They tell you it was nice to meet you, that you have an interesting résumé, and that they'll think about it and call you later. Which of the following is the response of a leader?

Response A: Oh, well, thank you so much for your time. I'll wait for your call. I look forward to hearing from you.

or

Response B: What's your timetable? I'm exploring several job opportunities that look good, and I'm wondering if you could give me some idea of when I could expect a response from you. Should I give you a call early next week?

What is the difference between these two responses?

Respondent A is being the effect. The interviewers are controlling the agenda, and Respondent A is dancing to their tune. Respondent B is driving the bus and forcing the employer to make some decisions. If you're Respondent B, you haven't done anything revolutionary, but you have said . . .

I'M NOT A GLOB OF SILLY PUTTY!

In effect, you have said, "I am not a shapeless substance to be formed by your needs, your schedule, and your agenda. I have my own shape and form. I am someone of substance. I am important. I value myself, and when we're discussing this job, we're interviewing each other. I need to know what I'm getting into just as much as you do. I am a leader."

Whew!

Did you say all that with your simple response?

Yes, you did. You acted like a leader. You said, I'm not whatever you want me to be; I am what I am. Doesn't that smack of leadership? Graciously and politely, you have said, This is what I am, and if it's not what you're looking for, that's fine—it means that this isn't right for me, either.

A follower needs to be dictated to by a given situation; that is the very definition of following. But a leader doesn't have that need. A leader will find the situation that suits her and won't slip into panic mode just because she's being evaluated for a job.

If you want to be a leader, resolve to be the cause, right now, in every situation. When you're the cause, nothing can stop you. You lead people and inspire them, and when you are totally acting as the cause in your life, the abundance you think you deserve will be dwarfed by what you will get. For leaders, the fulfillment and riches that await are limitless.

A Word About Certainty From The Russian Front

During World War II, after Germany invaded Russia, the United States sent an emissary to meet with the Russian forces to determine what role America should play in the war.

"General," the American asked, "how long will it take to expel the German army from your country?"

"I don't know," the Russian general replied.

"General," the American continued, "How many men do you think you will lose in repelling the invasion?"

"I don't know," the Russian again replied.

"General," the American said with some frustration, "you're the commander of the Russian forces, but you don't seem to know the most vital things about the war you're fighting."

It was the Russian's turn to speak.

"Okay," the general said, "Here's what I do know. I do know that however long I tell you the war is going to take, it will take longer than that. And that however many men I tell you it will require, it will require more than that. And I also know one more important thing: that whatever it costs and however long it takes, we will win in the end."

Such is the certainty of a leader—certainty of the outcome, yes, but along with it a willingness to let the process unfold. Leadership is a paradoxical mix of persistence and patience: A leader does everything in his power to produce the result right now, yet has enough wisdom to know that the Light is in the driver's seat—and to recognize that while the outcome is inevitable, its timetable will be determined by the Light.

A leader is powerful but doesn't force things. There are no explosions of impatience. As a leader, you will do everything in your power to follow the principles of true prosperity. You will be the boss. You will combat the negative effects of stress and fear; you will use ego properly. You will connect to Light consciousness; you will take on the mantle of certainty. You will use the entire spectrum of kabbalistic tools to achieve abundance and fulfillment.

You will also trust the process. You will know the end result but will let go of the outcome, knowing that the Light will guide you to true happiness, true fulfillment, and true prosperity.

NOW WHAT?

But before I leave you to enjoy your success, let me conclude with a few final words from those ancient business consultants, the kabbalists, for whom I'm happy to act as a messenger. These final words are like spark plugs: Apply them, and the principles you have learned in this book will ignite!

A BOAT THAT DOESN'T ROCK GOES NOWHERE

Practically everything is exactly the opposite of the way it appears. Another way of saying this is that our perceptions are so limited that we see the world upside down.

Another way of saying this is that every blessing is a curse and every curse a blessing.

When something starts off fraught with difficulty—when there are problems and disagreements and miscommunications—it's a good sign that the project will succeed. Conversely, when everything starts off easily—when you're amazed at how simple everything is—watch out, because that project probably won't pan out in the long run. It will certainly not be your gold mine.

Kabbalah tells us that when things are difficult, it means that some kind of Light is trying to be revealed.

HEARD OF THAT FORM OF COAL CALLED DIAMONDS?

You don't need to be in the jewelry business to know that a diamond equals coal + pressure. When one of the world's most plentiful, crude, and inexpensive substances —coal—is subjected to tons and tons of pressure, it is transformed from something worthless to the world's most precious jewel.

From this day on, as you conduct your business, you can elect to avoid trouble. You can dodge pressure, exit a situation when the going gets tough, and have your wife walk around with a nice piece of coal on her finger. Or you can choose to look closely as a project begins. Is it easy or difficult? Is it humming along smoothly, or is there chaos? If it's leaning toward the hard stuff, chances are there is a diamond waiting down the road with your name on it.

And now for the next spark plug . . .

Are You Willing To Ask For Help?

Once there was a great kabbalist who traveled with his students from town to town, staying wherever he could. One day he knocked on the door of a poor woodcutter, his wife, and three children. The family was so poor that they eked out an existence on the few pennies the man earned from woodcutting, and on the milk and cheese from a solitary cow in the backyard.

The woodcutter and his wife were honored to have the great kabbalist stay with them, and they invited him in. But once he was settled, the kabbalist proceeded to present them with an elaborate list of demands for dinner: meat courses, fish courses, salads, appetizers, desserts, and wine—a veritable banquet! The woodcutter and his wife were shocked by these demands—indeed, even the kabbalist's students were surprised—but the woodcutter and his wife complied. To provide the steak, they butchered their only cow, the source of all their milk and cheese. To pay for the rest of the elaborate meal - none of which they could afford—they began pulling wood from the house and selling it. When they were through, very little of their house remained.

Now the students were truly shocked. The poor woodcutter was left with no home and no source of food. Where did the kabbalist come off, destroying this man's life for the sake of personal enjoyment?

After the kabbalist left, the woodcutter sat down and pondered his fate. "I have nothing!" he cried aloud. In his desperation, he began asking the Light for help: "Light, please help me. I have nothing." Then he set off on the path through the woods, crying out to anyone he met: "Someone, please help me."

As the woodcutter walked through the forest, he ran into a man he had encountered now and then. The man informed him that his doctor had given him just a few months to live, and that everyone was bothering him because they knew he was quite wealthy. He complained that no one really cared about him. "But you," he said, looking closely at the woodcutter, "I've seen you now and then, and even though we don't know each other well, I have this strange feeling that you are truly a good man and that you love me. So I am going to leave everything I have to you."

Overnight, the woodcutter went from having nothing to being rich beyond his wildest dreams. He didn't understand it, but somehow he knew that the kabbalist had been involved in all this good fortune. So he set out in his gilded carriage to visit the kabbalist and personally thank him. The kabbalist's students were shocked to see the old woodcutter arrive in so fine a carriage, dressed in such elaborate clothing. And when the man finally put his question to the kabbalist, this was the reply:

"When your soul came into this world," the kabbalist told him, "You were destined for tremendous abundance and all the riches you could possibly want. But you were satisfied with that shack! You were content with milk and cheese from a tired old cow! When I took it all away from you, it forced you to ask for help. And the moment you asked for help, the abundance that should have been yours from the beginning made its presence known. All because you asked for help."

Perhaps you need to get rid of your shack and create room for the abundance you were destined to enjoy.

And maybe you need to ask for it.

WE ALL NEED HELP

Left to ourselves, we won't ask for help. And the irony here is that no matter how many times we read this book —no matter how ardently we work to apply any spiritual system, no matter how advanced our study of Kabbalah may be—if we're doing it Lone Ranger style, we will fail.

Sorry, but it's a law. When we go it alone, we go back to being selfish and plug back into reactive consciousness. But when we ask for help from the Light and from others and we honestly say, "I can't do this—please help me," then and only then can we get the assistance we need to win the war with ego, with selfish desires, with reactive consciousness, with trying to see the Big Picture of abundance rather than the hopelessness of the prison without walls.

So I urge you to do this program with a friend. Study these principles together and compare notes. Talk about the lessons. The more you talk and work with these ideas, the more they will become a part of you. Keep asking your friend questions, and have her ask you questions.

You can also ask help of The Kabbalah Centre. (You will find the numbers in the back of this book.) We have mentors you can call at any time to ask questions.

It is impossible to follow this system alone. America may be the country of rugged individualism, but to plug into

Light consciousness and to apply the spiritual laws of the universe, you need to experience the connection. We're all in this together.

So ask.

Ask for the abundance that is waiting for you.

Ask for the help of others on the journey.

But remember that in order to ask, you must first be open. You must feel that no matter how many advanced degrees you might have from MIT, or how many Nobel Prizes might be gracing your mantelpiece, you don't have all the answers. You must know that wisdom comes from unexpected places.

The following is a true story. In the early days of high-rise buildings, some architects were on a job site struggling to figure out where to put the emergency stairwell. Every place they suggested created a new problem for the floor plan. Just then, a janitor sweeping up near them overheard the conversation and asked, "Why don't you put the stairs outside the building?" The janitor then went on sweeping, and that building became the first one ever to have emergency stairs outside the building—still a common practice today.

It's important to accept it when someone comes to share with you. You don't have to take their advice, but you do need to be open. Be open enough to ask for advice; be open to asking help from the Light; and be open to receiving the Light. Be open to the possibility that someone could really give you what you need.

When we become channels for information and wisdom and the signals from the universe, we open the way for true prosperity to flow into our lives.

And now for the final spark plug . . .

Are You Excited Yet?

The spark plug of true prosperity is excitement. You must be excited about evolving if you want to maintain your forward momentum.

If you lose your excitement, it's difficult to stay successful. Without excitement, it's unlikely that you'll have great working relationships with other people. Without excitement, people keep looking at their watches rather than losing themselves in the thrill of making something new and wonderful happen.

The way to feel excited at work is to remember the first time you went to work, when everything was fresh and exciting to you. Remember when you were hired, or the day you started the company. Go back to the seeds, and have those seeds bloom again. Reinvigorate your work, and when you do—when you bring continual excitement into play—you will turn chaos into order. Nothing will seem like an obstacle, and nothing will be impossible.

So we're excited. We've opened our eyes to a different way of thinking, a different way to see money, a different way to see life, a different way to see business. But that initial excitement is not enough. We need to . . .

Wake Up!

We talk about excitement because it is the antidote to our biggest problem:

We are asleep.

Becoming the cause in our lives is the way to wake up. You can make a difference, and you will. Demand it of yourself. Your life full of true prosperity awaits. You have only to ask for it.

The End, Which Is Only The Beginning

There you have it—a recipe for abundance, tools to start using the second you close these pages. You now have what you need to build a spiritual company, if that is what you are called to do, or to build a life of success without side effects, if that is your goal.

Follow these principles. At first they will help you draw down more money from the universe, but they won't stop until you have more love, more joy, and more fulfillment than you ever imagined, and a world that works better for everyone else as well.

This is the power of true prosperity.

Demand it, take it, earn it, and enjoy it.

And let me know how it goes.

Thank you.

As part of an ongoing commitment to bring you technology that transforms lives, we're developing a Technology for the Soul coaching program over the phone. Soon, you will be able to work one-on-one with a dedicated Kabbalah coach who will assist you in applying this program in your life.

If you were inspired by this book in any way and would like to know how you can continue to enrich your life through the power of Kabbalah, here is what you can do next: Read the book *The Power of Kabbalah* or listen to *the Power of Kabbalah* audio tapes.

The Power of Kabbalah

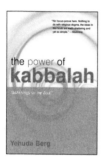

Imagine your life filled with unending joy, purpose, and contentment. Imagine your days infused with pure insight and energy. This is *The Power of Kabbalah*. It is the path from the momentary pleasure that most of us settle for, to the lasting fulfillment that is yours to claim. Your deepest desires are waiting to be realized.

But they are not limited to the temporary rush from closing a business deal, the short-term high from drugs, or a passionate sexual relationship that lasts only a few short months.

Wouldn't you like to experience a lasting sense of wholeness and peace that is unshakable, no matter what may be happening around you? Complete fulfillment is the promise of Kabbalah. Within these pages, you will learn how to look at and navigate through life in a whole new way. You will understand your purpose and how to receive the abundant gifts waiting for you. By making a critical transformation from a reactive to a proactive being, you will increase your creative energy, get control of your life, and enjoy new spiritual levels of existence. Kabbalah's ancient teaching is rooted in the perfect union of the physical and spiritual laws already at work in your life. Get ready to experience this exciting realm of awareness, meaning, and joy.

The wonder and wisdom of Kabbalah has influenced the world's leading spiritual, philosophical, religious, and scientific minds. Until today, however, it was hidden away in ancient texts, available only to scholars who knew where to look. Now after many centuries, *The Power of Kabbalah* resides right here in this one remarkable book. Here, at long last is the complete and simple path—actions you can take right now to create the life you desire and deserve.

The Power of Kabbalah Audio Tapes

The Power of Kabbalah is nothing less than a user's guide to the universe. Move beyond where you are right now to where you truly want to be—emotionally, spiritually, creatively. This exciting tape series brings you the ancient, authentic teaching of Kabbalah in a powerful, practical audio format.

You can order these products from our Web site or by calling Student Support.

More products that can help you bring the wisdom of Kabbalah into your life

The Red String Book: The Power of Protection
By Yehuda Berg

Read the book that everyone is *wearing!*

Discover the ancient technology that empowers and fuels the hugely popular Red String, the most widely recognized tool of kabbalistic wisdom. Yehuda Berg, author of the international best-seller *The 72 Names of God: Technology for the Soul,* continues to reveal the secrets of the world's oldest and most powerful wisdom with his new book, *The Red String Book: The Power of Protection.* Discover the antidote to the negative effects of the dreaded "Evil Eye" in this second book of the Technology for the Soul series.

Find out the real power behind the Red String and why millions of people won't leave home without it.

It's all here. Everything you wanted to know about the Red String but were afraid to ask!

The Dreams Book: Finding Your Way in the Dark
By Yehuda Berg

In *The Dreams Book*, the debut installment of the Technology for the Soul Series, national best-selling author Yehuda Berg lifts the curtain of reality to reveal secrets of dream interpretation that have remained hidden for centuries.

Readers will discover a millennia-old system for understanding dreams and will learn powerful techniques to help them find soul mates, discover career opportunities, be alerted to potential illness in the body, improve relationships with others, develop an overall deeper awareness, and much more.

The dream state is a mysterious and fascinating realm in which the rules of reality do not apply. This book is the key to navigating the dreamscape, where the answers to all of life's questions await.

God Wears Lipstick
By Karen Berg

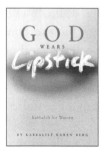

For 4,000 Years, Kabbalah was forbidden to women—until one woman decided that was long enough.

In directing Kabbalah Centres worldwide with her husband, Rav Berg, Karen Berg opened the world's most ancient form of wisdom to everyone on earth—for the first time.

Now, in *God Wears Lipstick*, she reveals women's special spiritual role in the universe.

Based on the wisdom of Kabbalah, *God Wears Lipstick* explains the spiritual advantage of women, the power of soulmates, and the true purpose of life, and conducts a no-holds-barred discussion of everything from managing relationships to reincarnation to the sacred power and meaning of sex.

The 72 Names of God: Technology for the Soul™
By Yehuda Berg

The story of Moses and the Red Sea is well known to almost everyone; it's even been an Academy Award–winning film. What is not known, according to the internationally prominent author Yehuda Berg, is that a state-of-the-art technology is encoded and concealed within that biblical story. This technology is called the 72 Names of God, and it is the key—your key—to ridding yourself of depression, stress, creative stagnation, anger, illness, and other physical and emotional problems. In fact, the 72 Names of God is the oldest, most powerful tool known to mankind—far more powerful than any 21st century high-tech know-how when it comes to eliminating the garbage in your life so that you can wake up and enjoy life each day. Indeed, the 72 Names of God is the ultimate pill for anything and everything that ails you because it strikes at the DNA level of your soul.

The power of the 72 Names of God operates strictly on a soul level, not a physical one. It's about spirituality, not religiosity. Rather than being limited by the differences that divide people, the wisdom of the Names transcends humanity's age-old quarrels and belief systems to deal with the one common bond that unifies all people and nations: the human soul.

Becoming Like God
By Michael Berg

At the age of 16, Kabbalistic scholar Michael Berg began the herculean task of translating *The Zohar*, Kabbalah's chief text, from its original Aramaic into its first complete English translation. *The Zohar*, which consists of 23 volumes, is considered a compendium of virtually all information pertaining to the universe, and its wisdom is only beginning to be verified today.

During the ten years he worked on *The Zohar*, Michael Berg discovered the long-lost secret for which mankind has searched for more than 5,000 years: how to achieve our ultimate destiny. *Becoming Like God* reveals the transformative method by which people can actually break free of what is called "ego nature" to achieve total joy and lasting life.

Berg puts forth the revolutionary idea that for the first time in history, an opportunity is being made available to humankind: an opportunity to Become Like God.

The Secret
By Michael Berg

Like a jewel that has been painstakingly cut and polished, *The Secret* reveals life's essence in its most concise and powerful form. Michael Berg begins by showing you how our everyday understanding of our purpose in the world is literally backwards. Whenever there is pain in our lives—indeed, whenever there is anything less than complete joy and fulfillment—this basic misunderstanding is the reason.

The Essential Zohar
By Rav Berg

The Zohar has traditionally been known as the world's most esoteric and profound spiritual document, but Kabbalist Rav Berg, this generation's greatest living Kabbalist, has dedicated his life to making this wisdom universally available. The vast wisdom and Light of *The Zohar* came into being as a gift to all humanity, and *The Essential Zohar* at last explains this gift to the world.

Power of You
By Rav Berg

For the past 5,000 years, neither science nor psychology has been able to solve the fundamental problem of chaos in people's lives.

Now, one man is providing the answer. He is Kabbalist Rav Berg.

Beneath the pain and chaos that disrupts our lives, Kabbalist Rav Berg brings to light a hidden realm of order, purpose, and unity. Revealed is a universe in which mind becomes master over matter—a world in which God, human thought, and the entire cosmos are mysteriously interconnected.

Join this generation's premier kabbalist on a mind-bending journey along the cutting edge of reality. Peer into the vast reservoir of spiritual wisdom that is Kabbalah, where the secrets of creation, life, and death have remained hidden for thousands of years.

Wheels of a Soul
By Rav Berg

In *Wheels of a Soul,* Kabbalist Rav Berg reveals the keys to answering these and many more questions that lie at the heart of our existence as human beings. Specifically, Rav Berg explains why we must acknowledge and explore the lives we have already lived in order to understand the life we are living today . . .

Make no mistake: *you have been here before.* Reincarnation is a fact—and just as science is now beginning to recognize that time and space may be nothing but illusions, Rav Berg shows why death itself is the greatest illusion of all.

In this book you learn much more than the answers to these questions. You will understand your true purpose in the world and discover tools to identify your life's soul mate. Read *Wheels of a Soul* and let one of the greatest kabbalistic masters of our time change your life forever.

THE KABBALAH CENTRE
The International Leader in the Education of Kabbalah

Since its founding, The Kabbalah Centre has had a single mission: to improve and transform people's lives by bringing the power and wisdom of Kabbalah to all who wish to partake of it.

Through the lifelong efforts of Kabbalists Rav and Karen Berg, and the great spiritual lineage of which they are a part, an astonishing 3.5 million people around the world have already been touched by the powerful teachings of Kabbalah. And each year, the numbers are growing!

Student Support: Trained instructors are available 18 hours a day. These dedicated people can answer any and all questions about Kabbalah free of charge and help guide you along in your effort to learn more. Just call **1-800-kabbalah.**

May we all have the merit to reconnect with a spiritual path and bring unity (a oneness) to the world.

Let this book enlighten us to the truth of prosperity and obtain a continuous abundance in our lives.

I wish health, happiness, & fulfillment to my parents Frances & Bernard, my sister Michele, and my brothers Robert & Kenneth.

Love & Light,

Paul Zuckerman